IT'S A
IRACLE

IT'S A
MIRACLE

REAL-LIFE INSPIRATIONAL
STORIES BASED ON
THE PAX TV SERIES
"IT'S A MIRACLE"
SELECTED BY

RICHARD THOMAS

A DELTA TRADE PAPERBACK

A Delta Book
Published by
Dell Publishing
a division of
Random House, Inc.
1540 Broadway
New York, New York 10036

Library of Congress Cataloging-in-Publication Data

It's a miracle: real-life inspirational stories based on the PAX TV
series It's a miracle / selected by Richard Thomas.
     p.   cm.
   ISBN 0-385-33650-0
   1. Miracles.   I. Thomas, Richard, 1951–   II. It's a miracle
(Television program)

BL487 .I87 2002
291.4'32—dc21

                                        2002025610

Manufactured in the United States of America

Published simultaneously in Canada

September 2002

10 9 8 7 6 5 4 3 2 1
BVG

CONTENTS

INTRODUCTION

In 1998, when I was asked to host a new show on PAX TV entitled *It's a Miracle,* I said to myself, "Great idea, but will anyone really care about all of this 'good news'?"

Well, four years and hundreds of stories later, I have my answer: people LOVE good news; and, yes, they DO care.

And I care. Every week, I have gotten pleasure and spiritual sustenance from bringing these wonderful true stories to the television audience. I am very happy now to bring them to you in book form, and I hope they will touch you as much as they've touched me.

In this selection of favorite stories from *It's a Miracle,* you will read of soul mates brought together after years and miles of separation, and of medical recoveries for which there are no apparent medical explanations. You will learn about astonishing rescues and read stories that literally involve the gift of life—organ donations and transplants. You will also enjoy heartwarming animal stories, which always delight me, because I'm such an animal lover.

I hope these stories will give you goose bumps. The people in them were from all walks of life, living ordinary lives, when something extraordinary happened—something they have all described as miraculous.

I hope these stories will lift up your heart and give you faith in humanity. They may also make you cry. They have done all those things for me.

They may even help you to look at your own life differently, as they show that miracles really can happen. Anytime. Anywhere. And to anyone.

Happy reading.

—RICHARD THOMAS

IT'S A
MIRACLE

ROMANTIC PROVIDENCE

FIRST LOVE

The Great Depression hit Otto Sloan's family, like so many others, hard. When his parents separated, Otto was sent to live with grandparents in Colorado. But soon, economic hardships once again forced Otto to move.

"Back when I was, oh, ten or eleven years old, my grandparents sent me to live with and work for Mrs. Rowan and her husband. So I went there to help and worked there with them. And I did that for some time," recalls Otto.

It was while living there that he met Betty Jean Hodge, the daughter of a neighboring farmer.

"My earliest recollection," says Betty Jean, "was when

I'd get on the school bus, and he'd be on the bus, already there. And then he would look up at me, with a kind of smile in his eyes."

"She was a very pretty girl, I thought," says Otto. "And I wanted to speak to her then. But I didn't. I was very bashful, you might say. I never would look at her direct, into her face or anything like that. I always cast my eyes down. I still do that to this day."

As the years passed, Otto's and Betty's paths continued to cross.

"There were occasions when Otto would come down with the horse and he would round up the cattle," says Betty Jean, "and I would always beg him to let me ride the horse."

Otto wasn't sure about that, however. "I said, 'No, the horse is a one-man horse,'" recalls Otto. "I said, 'It'd be better if you didn't.'"

But Betty Jean persevered. "I had asked him and pleaded with him so much that Dad finally said, 'Otto, you might as well let her on it, because she won't give up until you do.'"

"So he was hoisting me up on the horse," says Betty Jean. "And he wasn't sure just how to go about doing that, because he was afraid he might touch me in an immodest place on my body. He was very careful of that," she remembers, laughing. "He wanted to be precise in getting me on the horse."

"So I finally ended up making a stirrup out of my hands, and had her put her foot in it," says Otto. "I raised her up that way—and the horse just flew, it seemed to me, full blast for home.

"I hollered at her, 'Drop the reins, drop the reins!' She wouldn't drop the reins," Otto says, laughing. "If she would've dropped them, the horse would've stopped."

The horse finally came to a stop at the end of the field.

"And I looked up at Betty, and you could see that there was fright in her eyes," recalls Otto.

"I kind of leaned over and he put his arms around my waist," adds Betty Jean. "And I think I was probably trembling a little bit. He said, 'It's all right, you're all right.' And then he took me back home," she laughs.

From that day on, Betty and Otto were inseparable.

"I thought our relationship at that time . . . he was kind of like a big brother to me. Then in 1941 we started dating. And our dating meant going to basketball games together, or roller-skating," says Betty Jean.

As their dates continued, Otto's and Betty Jean's feelings for each other deepened.

"We'd been roller-skating several times together, and a friend of mine then had a little Model A with a rumble seat in it," says Otto. "Well, Betty and I were in the back in the rumble seat, and I reached over and kissed her. I really felt that that was what was supposed to be done. And that's what I did," he chuckles.

"I'll never forget the emotions I felt when he kissed me. He held me close and kissed me so gently," says Betty Jean. "And that just stayed with me for years. I never forgot it."

But the love that was blossoming between them was suddenly interrupted by the outbreak of World War II. And like so many other young men, Otto followed the call to battle.

"The last time I saw him, he came down to our place," Betty Jean remembers. "To see him go, it felt like I'd never see him again.

"It was hard. It was hard to see him go."

"I went into the navy in July of 1941. And they shipped us out of San Diego after we finished training, to Pearl Harbor," says Otto.

It was there that Otto would come face-to-face with the horror of war. On December 7, 1941, hundreds of Japanese bombers attacked the island in two waves of destruction.

By the time the surprise attack ended two hours later, 21 ships were destroyed and over 2,400 people lay dead. Otto's division of 122 sailors did not escape unscathed.

"There were only seventy-some of us left. So I lost a lot of good friends at that time. It was quite a blow," says Otto.

The only thing that helped ease the pain was Betty Jean's letters.

"And though he wasn't much of a writer, I would write constantly because I felt it was important to keep his morale up," says Betty Jean. "I would write about incidents that happened, the funny things that happened, and I would send jokes and letters and things."

The letters kept their love alive during the lonely

months at sea. And then, just before Betty Jean graduated from high school, a special package arrived.

Betty Jean recalls, laughing, "I was practically tearing it apart on my way to the house. I got to the house and opened it up, and there was a little jewelry box, and inside the box there was a string of pearls. My first reaction was that he must have thought a lot of me to get me a string of pearls," says Betty Jean. "It meant a lot to me to think that he cared that much, and I think that it was his way of trying to tell me something that he ... that he just couldn't express in words."

Betty Jean was right. Otto was in love and he was ready to ask for her hand in marriage. He eventually wired her to meet him in California when he returned to the States on leave, so that they could finalize their plans.

"But then her dad said no. He said, 'I don't think you should do that,'" says Otto. "I was really upset at the time about it."

"I was very, very disappointed that I didn't get to see him then," says Betty Jean. "After that was when things began to slow down a little bit. I didn't hear quite so often from him after he went back to sea."

As the war intensified, and Otto's letters stopped arriving, Betty Jean feared the worst.

"I had thought that he had been killed, because I hadn't heard anything from him after that. So," she says, emotionally, "I felt like he was gone. I felt that way for years."

As the war in the Pacific stretched from months into years, Otto made the difficult decision to stop writing his girlfriend so that she could get on with her life. And when the letters stopped coming, Betty Jean had no choice but to face the facts.

"When I came to the realization that I would probably never see Otto again, I realized that life would have to go on, though I hadn't heard from him. And I began to date others," she says. "Then I met my husband, Clarence, and we married and had five children."

As the years passed, Betty Jean would often wonder what had happened to Otto.

"He was always there in the back of my mind, like a piece of my heart that had been tucked away and hidden for a while," she reflects.

Life continued for Betty Jean, and in June of 1995, she and Clarence celebrated their fiftieth wedding anniversary.

"The years just literally flew by, and then came the time when I lost my husband. He'd been ill for some time. And then, my thoughts went to Otto. I could not get him out of my mind, wondering if he were alive. Just wishing I could hear something," Betty Jean says.

And then, as if someone heard her prayer, Betty Jean received a letter from one of Otto's cousins, Lila, with an old photograph inside.

"It had my three sisters and me in it, and it was taken in 1938," she describes. "A grade school picture."

"I was so excited and so exhilarated when I got that, that I just had to get in touch with Lila and thank her for it," recalls Betty Jean. "And I said, 'Incidentally, have you ever heard from your cousin Otto?'"

And in reply, Cousin Lila sent her Otto's phone number.

Betty Jean called him up, saying, "Otto Sloan? This is a gal that you probably won't remember."

"And I couldn't believe it, but I recognized her voice," declares Otto. "It's Betty Jean," he said.

"How did you know who it was?" she laughed.

"I'd recognize that voice anyplace," Otto replied.

The call could not have come at a more perfect time, for Otto had also lost his wife of nearly fifty years. And he too had never forgotten his first love. Soon they were writing and talking on a daily basis, and fifty-eight years of separation quickly vanished.

"You just don't realize how many times I've wondered where you were and what you were doing. And if you were all right," Betty Jean told Otto. "You're probably looking just as young as you ever did.

"And then the talks got a little more personal," Betty Jean reveals. "We told each other our strengths and weaknesses.

"We just talked about everything there was to talk about. It was just like we were face-to-face," she laughs. "And then it became apparent that we were discussing marriage possibilities."

"It was unbelievable that we could feel so much love for each other just by talking on the phone like we had," says Otto.

"We had made definite plans just over the phone, practically. We're getting married. If anybody had been there to pronounce us man and wife, we would've accepted that," laughs Betty Jean.

In the summer of 1999, after not seeing each other for fifty-eight years, Otto and Betty Jean were reunited.

"My heart was pounding so hard that I could hardly keep it in its place," says Betty Jean, laughing. "He just took my hand and hung on to it for dear life. And I whispered to him, 'Don't ever let go of me again. Don't ever let go of me again.' And he said, 'Don't worry, I won't.'"

Otto kept his promise four weeks later when he pledged to take Betty Jean as his lawful wedded wife, to have and to hold, from this day forward, so long as they both should live.

"Betty Jean is still the little girl that I used to love, and still love," says Otto.

"He's the same as he was when he was a boy," says Betty Jean. "And I've even told him that. I said, 'You look just like you were.' When he puts his head down and looks up at me like that, I just see him all over again, sitting there on that school bus when I'd get on the bus. I probably wasn't sure at the time what that really meant, but I found out later—fifty-eight years later," she laughs.

"And we feel that our getting back together was a miracle; our lives are like a dream. It's something that you just maybe would dream of but not ever expect to happen."

She adds, laughing, "I think we're living happily ever after."

HIGH SCHOOL REUNION

It was 1975, and Jenna Hamburger was a seventh-grade student in Fair Lawn, New Jersey. And, like most thirteen-year-old girls, Jenna was beginning to discover boys.

"My first crush was on a boy named Marc Meltzer," explains Jenna. "He was one of the smartest kids I knew. He was also adorable. He had blondish-reddish hair and freckles. He was just the kind of person that made you feel good to be around.

"And we had classes together. I would write notes to my girlfriends about him, how cute I thought he was. I used to tell my mom I was going out bike riding, I'd be back in an hour. And I would always go down Marc's street, just to see if he was outside, maybe mowing the lawn. And my heart would always pound if I happened to see him. And that's what I remember about discovering the opposite sex," Jenna laughs.

By the time she was a senior, Jenna had all but forgotten her first crush. But Marc Meltzer still had a soft spot in his heart for this young girl. And so, just before graduation, he gave her his class picture, along with a personal note.

"And then we sort of lost touch," says Jenna. "I had no idea what had happened to him. And that was about it."

Jenna and Marc went their separate ways. She enrolled in a local college, while he attended a school in Virginia.

Nine years later, Marc was back in Fair Lawn, running his father's sales agency. But the hard work and long hours left little time for a love life.

"The business that I'm in," explains Marc, "I don't really have an office of people that I can socialize with: 'Hey, I know somebody, why don't you go out with them?' My sister had asked me at that time, 'Why don't you put an ad in *New York* magazine?' And I thought about it for a minute, and I said, 'Well, you know what? Why not? Give it a shot.' So I sat down, and over a few days I composed an ad. It read: 'Call your mother. You've just found that nice Jewish boy she's always told you about. I live in New Jersey, but I've been looking for you everywhere. On ski slopes, at the movies, in Chinese restaurants . . .' And at that point, I didn't tell anyone. I didn't want people to think of me as, 'Here's a loser who can't find some girl on his own. He's going to go to a personal ad.'"

But Marc was not prepared for the response he received from his ad.

"When I went to the mailbox," Marc says, "I found not one or two letters, but ten letters in the first packet that came to me. And I couldn't believe it. For someone who didn't date a lot, here I was in a situation where I had three dates booked on one weekend. I had a Friday night date, a Saturday lunch date, and a Saturday night date, which was a totally foreign experience for me."

Marc ended up dating six of the women who'd written him. But none of them had that special "spark" he was looking for. And eventually, the letters, and his interest in them, began to dwindle.

Meanwhile, Jenna Hamburger was a world away living in Philadelphia, Pennsylvania.

"I got myself a job working at a law firm in Center City," recounts Jenna. "I was on my lunch hour. We always had a selection of magazines to look through. I happened to pick up the *New York* magazine, and I started reading the personals, as I would do from time to time. I didn't really specifically think I would answer one. However, I saw this one ad that really spoke to me."

She adds, "The person seemed to have a sense of humor and be down to earth, and I thought, This is a person that I could possibly have a lot in common with and get along with. I wrote a letter to the person, which difficult. I had never done it before. And I hoped that he wouldn't think it was strange that I was living in Philadelphia and answering an ad from New York. And then I just tried to forget about it, because I didn't even know if this person I was writing to would respond to me."

A few days later, Jenna's letter arrived.

"The envelope had a return address of Philadelphia," Marc says, "which was unusual because most of the responses were from the New York tristate area. She signed her name Jenna, at the bottom, and as soon as I looked at that handwriting, I said to myself, I know this person. This is Jenna Hamburger. This is Jenna Hamburger from Fair Lawn. This is Jenna Hamburger that I went to school with. And this is fantastic. Because Jenna was someone who I liked. I hadn't seen her since that time I gave her my yearbook photo. But I liked her in seventh and eighth grade."

Marc immediately picked up the phone to give her a call.

"It was the day before Valentine's Day, and I wanted to call her right then and there. I was very excited to do that," says Marc.

"Hi, Jenna. I'm the guy whose ad you answered in *New York* magazine," Marc introduced himself.

"And my heart started pounding because I obviously wasn't prepared for this. I couldn't believe he was calling," says Jenna.

"Jenna," continued Marc, "when I put that ad in, people asked me if I ever got a response from someone I know. And I know you."

"I started to get very nervous," recalls Jenna. "My heart was pounding. I'm thinking, Who could this be that knows me? Here I'm living in Philadelphia, I'm answering an ad in *New York* magazine, and I'm answering the ad of somebody I knew."

"So," continues Marc, "I told Jenna, 'I know you. I grew up with you. We went to elementary school together. We went to junior high school together.' And then I heard a gasp on the other side."

"I knew right away it was Marc Meltzer," says Jenna. "Who I hadn't seen in ten years."

Adds Marc, "It was an amazing moment. And, um, at that time, we made a date."

Two weeks later they met face-to-face.

"I was very excited," Marc remembers. "I was excited when I drove out there. I was excited to see Jenna. It was as if no time had passed."

"We hugged and just started talking," says Jenna. "It really wasn't awkward. And before he left to go home, he asked if he could see me the following weekend. So I knew right then and there that he was definitely as interested in me as I was interested in him."

"Basically, I knew at that point that I wasn't going to be calling up the forty-three other girls who had sent responses to me," admits Marc. "This was going to be it. I'm going to pursue this relationship with Jenna."

But Jenna and Marc's chance encounter was about to take an even more amazing turn.

"We were looking through her photo albums—Jenna has a photo basically of every minute of her life—and as we were looking through the yearbook, Jenna found my old picture," Marc recounts. "She looks at it and says, 'Oh, that's a goofy picture.' You know, 'Look how silly you look in high school.' "

"It was the custom back then to trade pictures," explains Jenna, "and you would write a very meaningful message on the back of the picture before you gave it to your friend."

"And she turned it over," continues Marc, "and that's when she saw what I had written ten years ago. It said, 'Let's make a pact and meet again in ten years.' And it was something I had forgotten I had written. I don't know what the connection was, why I had even written that in high school. It was just some goofy thing. But, uh, we looked at the calendar, and sure enough, it was almost ten years from when I had given her that photo that we hooked up again."

Fifteen months later they became hooked together for life as husband and wife.

"I took a chance on love by answering this ad," concludes Jenna. "And it worked out in the best way possible. It's hard for me to really explain how this happened. How out of all the hundreds of ads that were in the magazine, I answered his ad. I just have to believe that it was fate. That we were meant to be together. And after all those years of being apart, this was the way that we were meant to be back together."

WRONG NUMBER MARRIAGE

Dana Herring and Dennis Dunbar first met in 1973 while attending high school in Los Angeles. At the time, they were just casual friends.

"After initially meeting Dana, I just felt that she had no interest in me," remembers Dennis. "So I felt that it was just something that would not be worthwhile pursuing."

"Dennis was going out with a friend of mine, and I was going out with another person," recalls Dana. "It was just not convenient."

But nine years later, Dennis and Dana met again, at the wedding of mutual friends. And this time, the chemistry between them was different.

"I thought he looked pretty handsome in his tuxedo," says Dana. "There was an attraction that night at the wedding, and we talked for a long time. We ended up pretty much staying together that whole night at the wedding. And that was it."

"We had a good time, and we just enjoyed each other's company," agrees Dennis.

Dana and Dennis began dating, and over the next few months their romance blossomed. As it became more serious, they made plans to go away together for Memorial Day weekend. But before he picked her up for their getaway, Dennis stopped by the home of his newlywed friends.

It was a decision that would change all his plans.

"This girl had come down from San Francisco," Dennis recalls, "and they wanted to set me up with her. They knew that I was going out with Dana, but they probably didn't realize how serious the relationship was at the time.

"They talked me into breaking my date with Dana," Dennis says.

Dana, understandably, was quite upset. "I was upset because we did have plans. And, you know, he called at the last minute to cancel," she says. "I was really angry at the time. I just hung up on him, and that was it."

"She didn't deserve that," says Dennis. "And I felt like an idiot. I never talked to Dana after that."

Dennis ended up marrying the woman who was his blind date that day. But after ten years together the marriage failed, and in 1997, Dennis was once again a bachelor.

At that time, Dennis owned his own pest control business, and on Labor Day 1997, he was sitting in his office, calling clients to confirm appointments for the following day.

"There was one customer in particular that I called, left a message that I'd be out tomorrow to take care of her account, left my name and my phone number like I always do, and said if there's any problem call me back," recalls Dennis. "The next day I went out to service the account, and for some weird reason, the customer had never gotten my message."

But someone else had.

"I came home from out of town, checked my messages, and one of them struck me as strange," remembers Dana, "because it was from a man, and he said, 'Hello, Terry, this is Dennis Dunbar calling from Dunbar Pest Control.' And I thought the voice sounded very familiar."

"That evening the phone rang," says Dennis, "and it turned out to be a girl who asked if this was the Dennis Dunbar who has a brother named Dan, which I do."

Dana recalls, "And I said, 'This is Dana Herring.'"

Dennis was shocked to hear from her, and asked how she got his number. "And she said, 'Well, you called me,'" he remembers. "And it hit me, Wait a second! This other customer didn't get the message I left. So I got my customer's card and I repeated the number, which had a 960 prefix. At which point Dana said, 'How funny. That's very close to mine. Mine is 906.'"

He had transposed two numbers. "What a coincidence," said Dennis.

"I was literally shaking," he recalls.

"One of the first things she said after we chitchatted a bit," Dennis remarks, "was, 'If I remember it right, didn't you stand me up?' And I was like, 'Well, but that was a long time ago. I hope you're not still mad,'" he chuckles.

"And he said, 'You do remember what happened?'" says Dana. "And I said, 'Yes, I do remember.' I said, 'You broke a date with me, and then you married her,'" she laughs.

Dennis told her about his divorce, and Dana revealed to him that she'd never gotten married.

"So we talked a little bit longer, and I was saying how weird this was," Dennis says. "She said, 'Well, if you like, you can give me a call sometime, and maybe we can get together.'" Dennis told her he'd love to, and that was the end of that conversation.

"When he called me the next day at my office, between ten and eleven in the morning, and my secretary said, 'Dennis Dunbar is on the phone,' I was shocked," says Dana. "I was like, Well, gosh, he's already calling? We set a date for Friday night, and he showed up with flowers, and we sat and talked for about four hours when we were supposed to go out to dinner."

"I haven't talked to somebody like the way I talk to Dana for years," declares Dennis. "It just really felt good. It was completely different than any relationship I had ever been in. . . . It felt like it was meant to be."

"We feel that we were brought together for a special reason," Dana proclaims.

And thirteen months later, Dennis and Dana became husband and wife. For them, their marriage is nothing less than a miracle.

"The miracle is how the whole thing happened," says Dana. "How he happened to transpose that one number and reach me of all people, out of ten million people in Los Angeles."

"Timing was everything in this, because the area codes had already changed out there," says Dennis. "If I had dialed that number two months later, I don't think I ever would have run across Dana again."

"I think I'm probably the happiest I've ever been in my entire life right now. I am just glowing," says Dana.

"It's heaven," agrees Dennis. "You know, this is the person that I'm going to be with for the rest of my life, and I'm looking forward to it."

$\mathcal{A}$CTING UPON FATE

From the time she was a young girl growing up in Oklahoma, Cyndi Steele was stagestruck. But it wasn't only the lights and costumes that fascinated her. She had a mad crush on one of the local actors, nineteen-year-old Chris Harrod.

"She was always there," recalls Chris. "She had these little glasses on and little braces. She was just really cute, and I remember thinking, What a cute kid."

In 1992, Cyndi left Oklahoma for New York City to pursue her dream of acting, and it paid off when she landed a role in a stage production of *Bye Bye Birdie*.

"It was kinda cool to get a chorus thing right off,"

Cyndi says. "'Cause I didn't do that kinda work. And I thought, All I can do is get older and do the character roles, so this was great."

But during a preview performance, a freak accident changed all her plans.

"We were just standing in the wings," recounts Cyndi, "waiting to go on for bows, and a friend in the show just flips his head back, and it just knocked me right above my right eye. Instead of falling body first, I fell head first. The back of my head stopped my fall."

Cyndi was knocked unconscious. None of the actors could revive her. When she finally regained consciousness, she was in a hospital.

Cyndi says, "A nurse came up to me, and she said that I had fallen and hit my head. And I said, 'Where?' She said, 'At work. You were doing a show.' And she said, 'Your friends are out there.' She opened the door, and they're just waving at me enthusiastically . . . and I have no idea who they are.

"So I came back from the hospital," Cyndi continues. "I saw there were photos of my family, and I didn't know exactly who everybody was. . . . I knew my name was Cyndi Steele, but that didn't make any sense to me. Nothing made any sense."

Cyndi was suffering from severe amnesia brought on by blunt head trauma and a concussion. Unable to remember the simplest things, she began staying at home, alone, isolated from an unfamiliar world.

"I found some journals, and I thought they would help me piece things together. They were disjointed, but it helped.

There were still so many gaps," Cyndi explains. "And I didn't want to meet people. It was too frustrating."

A worried friend finally convinced Cyndi to join her for a night out. As they sat watching a movie, Cyndi noticed that something about the man sitting next to her seemed familiar.

"And I just kinda looked at him," remembers Cyndi, "and I said, 'Did I know you before?' And he was like, 'Yeah, I'm Chris Harrod.'"

"We were watching the movie, having a great time," Chris adds, "and the whole time, I'm thinking, This is strange. . . . I'm starting to be attracted to somebody who I've known since they were twelve. Who doesn't remember who I am. This is really weird."

A few days later, Chris spent an evening with Cyndi talking about his acting career and how it had brought him to New York. But he didn't bring up the past. As far as Cyndi knew, she was meeting him for the first time. Chris was very moved by how hard she tried to act like nothing was wrong.

"Now, I just thought that she was really brave and strong, and I thought, I'm gonna sit here as long as she'll let me. And then we were just together, we were inseparable," says Chris.

A few weeks later, Cyndi returned to Oklahoma, hoping her parents could help fill in the gaps in her life.

"And I said, 'I'm seeing this guy. His name is Chris Harrod,'" recalls Cyndi. "And they just about choked, because the psychiatrist told them, 'Don't bring up her past. Just be open to what she's doing—as hard as that will be for you.'"

And so Cyndi's parents kept quiet. Then one afternoon, while paging through a scrapbook, she found pictures of the man she'd left behind in New York.

"The more I dig, I find picture after picture of Chris," exclaims Cyndi. "Cutouts with 'I love you' or 'You're so cute' written on them. And I'm just laughing, and when I open the door, my parents are laughing, 'cause they were dying to tell me this forever."

They told her how she used to hang around the community theater, watching her dad perform...and always hoping to get a glimpse of Chris. The story jogged her memory, and suddenly she remembered how she'd once told her parents that, one day, she would marry Chris Harrod.

"It was just like something clicked. I just went to the phone and called him, and I was like, 'I was totally in love with you,' " Cyndi recounts.

Chris adds, "And I thought, This is fate. This is what it is, this is fate. I mean, you don't just meet somebody and then have this happen and not automatically think that there's something special going on here."

Chris's prediction came true on December 22, 1995. And today, the happy couple has added another little miracle to their life: their son, Dalton. Even though Cyndi has recovered only thirty percent of her long-term memory, she believes that she has enough good memories to last her a lifetime.

"The few I have," confirms Cyndi, "I'll treasure them. I wouldn't change it. Something good came out of that accident."

MIRACLE REUNION

When Elsa Amador was twelve years old and living in Puerto Rico, she met a young boy who was the son of Roberto Clemente, the legendary baseball player who had been tragically killed in a plane crash. Elsa and Roberto junior instantly felt a strong attraction to each other.

"We told each other we loved each other every day.... I mean, every day, like twenty-five times a day," says Elsa.

In spite of their tender age, Roberto and Elsa believed they would spend their lives together. But a tragic event tore them apart. Elsa's father was the innocent victim of a botched robbery attempt. And now, his family was in extreme danger.

Elsa's mother had identified the man who killed her husband and was receiving death threats. The FBI moved in to take control of the situation. Elsa had only enough time to briefly call Roberto before she and her family were rushed out of the country, into the Witness Protection Program.

"I explained to him that we had to leave," Elsa recounts. "Unfortunately, I couldn't tell him where we were going. I just kept telling him how much I cared for him and not to blame me for what I was going to do. . . . It was out of my control."

Elsa spent the next few years moving around the United States. But she never forgot her childhood sweetheart.

"I thought about him all the time," Elsa admits. "I would sometimes close my eyes and see an image of him. He was really thin and tall and just smiling all the time. As time went on, I sort of assumed he had his own life. I just imagined him settled and married. . . ."

In November of 1996, Elsa's mother was diagnosed with terminal cancer. She had always felt responsible for separating her daughter from her childhood sweetheart. On her deathbed in the hospital, she made a startling request, urging Elsa to find her lost love.

"Find Roberto," Elsa's mother told her. "He's the man for you."

"So I asked, 'How am I going to find him?' And she said, 'You should find him.' And so I kind of brushed it off," says Elsa.

And then, a few months after her mother's death, Elsa had a sudden, unexplainable urge to attend a Yankees baseball game.

"It was as if something was just pushing me," describes Elsa.

Whatever was pushing Elsa to the stadium, got her there an hour early that day—just in time for a pre-game event. The Yankees were celebrating Hispanic Heritage Day, and there in center field, accepting an award for his father, was Elsa's long lost love—Roberto Clemente, Jr.

"It was really strange," Elsa recalls with wonder. "I thought, What is he doing there? I haven't seen him for all of these years and all of a sudden I see him at the park."

After the ceremony, Roberto disappeared from the field. Elsa spent the next nine innings of the game desperately trying to locate him, but without success. The boy she had never forgotten...the man her mother begged her to find...was closer than he'd ever been in over fifteen years, and still he was out of reach. Finally, a security guard gave her a possible lead, the phone number of a local sports café. Elsa called and left a message, and the next day Roberto returned the call and arranged to meet again the woman he had been separated from so many years ago.

"I felt like I had just seen her yesterday," declares Roberto. "Like I had just been with her in school the day before. And the feelings that I had for Elsa were so strong. My friends, everybody, knew about Elsa. It was something that I just...I kept her alive in my heart."

On Valentine's Day, 1998, Roberto and Elsa made

their reunion complete when they married in New York City. Today, they still marvel over how powers far beyond their own made the dying wish of Elsa's mother come true.

"I truly believe that our parents had a meeting in heaven and said, 'Wait a second...let's do something here,'" Roberto says. "I believe that it was meant to be, and I truly believe that it was a time where our parents' souls got together and said, 'Let's just make our two children happy.'"

For Roberto and Elsa, a tragic separation has ended happily with a miraculous second chance.

THE SPIRIT OF STRENGTH

JUMPING LIFE'S HURDLES

As a collegiate athlete, John Register was at the top of his form. He ran on four championship teams at the University of Arkansas and held three all-American titles in track-and-field.

"I had a great year in 1987, but in 1988 I really put my athletic career on hold to get my degree and get out of school. So my track-and-field career suffered a little bit during that time."

After graduation, John married his childhood sweetheart, Alice Johnson, and they soon became the proud parents of a son, John Register, Jr. But it was the dream of Olympic gold that led John to the U.S. Army and their world-class athlete training program. His road to the Olympics, however, would soon take an unexpected detour.

"I got called up to serve in the Gulf War. And so I went and served with the 5th and 27th Field Artillery in Operation Desert Storm."

Seven months later, John returned from the war and resumed his quest for the Olympic gold. But with only limited training time available, he failed to make the 1992 team.

"I wasn't dejected by that at all, and I started calculating almost immediately. I said, If I can just improve three places each year, I can be on that team in 1996."

So he intensified his training, and his performance steadily improved. It seemed his dream would become a reality...until the end of one fateful training session.

"I decided to take one more pass down the track before shutting it down. I was just too tired to save my energy for the next day."

He cleared each of the hurdles with room to spare, until suddenly he fell short.

"I knew it was going to be difficult to make the thirteen steps for the next hurdle, but I got across it, and when I landed my leg popped out of the socket. I saw that my left leg was crossed over my right leg with my foot pointing back toward my face. And I just turned away from it. I couldn't look at it anymore. Then the pain hit. It was tremendous. I felt like the whole leg was just on fire, was just exploding."

John was taken to the Wesley Medical Center in Wichita, Kansas. Alice and John junior rushed to his side.

Alice remembers, "When I walked in I didn't see my husband. I saw a man, but he didn't look like John. . . . It was as if every muscle from head to toe were hurting."

Doctors discovered that John's popliteal artery had been severed, preventing blood from circulating to his lower leg. Gangrene had set in, forcing them to remove the infected muscle tissue from his calf, but John's prognosis was bleak.

Alice says, "The doctor said, 'You can keep your leg and you will walk with severe pain and a limp for the rest of your life, or we can amputate your leg and you can re-build your life. It's not a decision I need right now, but we're gonna need it soon.'"

John says, "I knew that it had to come off. I just knew that it had to be done. The answer was clear. Let's get rid of the pain, and then we can deal with the other stuff later. I could not see myself living with either a wheelchair or a walker and being in pain. Especially the pain that I was feeling at that point in my life."

Once again John was taken into surgery, this time to amputate his leg above the knee.

"About three days after the amputation," Alice remembers, "I asked him if he was strong enough to get up and if he would like to go outside."

"I said, 'Well, just park the wheelchair right here and I'll just watch you all playing on the swings,'" says John. "And when I saw that I could not get out of that chair and go over with John junior to the swing and the slide, I actually understood what it meant to be different—to be a changed individual. And I think that's when the limitations started piling on me. I think I started to realize that I wasn't going to the Olympic trials. This dream was over for me. I would never run again."

"I heard John just crying," remembers Alice. "Just crying. So I walked back over and John junior walked over and we just hugged him. And I think at that moment John really realized that his leg was gone."

Having accepted his loss, John focused on rebuilding his life, attacking his therapy with the same dedication that had made him a world-class athlete.

John says, "In my mind, I was ready to start the recovery process. And I didn't really know what to expect at that point. But I knew that whatever I had to do, I had to get strong again."

Determined to strengthen his body, John began swimming. His competitive instincts soon took over. One year after his accident, John made the U.S. swim team and competed in the 1996 Paralympic Games in Atlanta.

John remembers, "That's where I think the idea was sparked in my head to come back to the sport of my first love, track-and-field."

John immediately started training to run in the 2000 Sydney Paralympic Games. His results, however, were not encouraging.

"I'd go out there and strap the leg on and run down the track. I was trying to get the rhythm and it just wasn't coming."

Alice remembers, "After a run, the skin would be gone

on the inner part of his leg. And he would have large sores on it."

John says, "And I said, 'Well, maybe I can't do this.' The doubt started creeping in."

But Alice and John made a pact that would help John get back out on the track.

Alice says, "I was learning to rollerblade and I had severely twisted my ankle. And I said, 'I'm not getting back on another rollerblade.'"

Alice agreed to try rollerblading again if John would try running 100 meters.

John remembers, "She used the rollerblades to show me that if she could go back to it even though she was so scared of them, then I could get up there and get on my leg and run again as well."

Alice says, "So we did it together. I rollerbladed the 100 and he ran for 100. And at that point I was excited. I could see his joy in it again."

A few days later, John ran his first competitive race since losing his leg.

"It was the scariest thing I had ever done. I mean, I had no control. I saw the backs of almost every athlete out there. And I was just fighting to stay upright, to stay balanced and not to fall, but at the same time, when I crossed that line I said to myself, You know, you just did it. You just ran against the best of the world here."

Two weeks later, John qualified for the Disabled World Championships in the 100 meters and the long jump. Still, he knew he could do better.

"The leg was whipping around and it was not working

with my body. I was actually fighting it. When I ran, I was landing on the top portion of the leg. And that was cutting into the inside groin area. So every time I landed, the pain was so bad that I felt like I was on fire."

But someone was watching who would change John's life forever: a prosthetic designer named Tom Guth.

Tom says, "His speed was incredible, fantastic, but his leg was just whipping to the side and going in all directions. And I thought, What a shame. This man has so much power, so much speed. If we could straighten his leg out and get him a good fit, he could probably be a gold medal winner."

Using advanced technology at the RGP Prosthetic Research Center in San Diego, Tom designed a new state-of-the-art running-and-jumping prosthetic for John.

"The results were just phenomenal," John remembers. "Two seconds had just come off of my time. And I felt my body come back to me again. It was an incredible feeling and I knew I was going to make the U.S. team for the Paralympic Games, so I could compete in Sydney, Australia."

The first step was the qualifying trials.

John says, "I saw myself on that runway and the competitive spirit just came back. I thought, You know what to do, you've been in this position many times before, and you can do it."

And he did.

John's Olympic dreams had come true. In spite of all the suffering and hardship, he was competing once again.

"It was a dream come true," John says. "And even though I'm not on the track as an able-bodied athlete, having the experience of playing at the Games is better. It's been really fantastic to understand that you can push your body to another level."

John posted a personal best in every event he competed in, winning a silver medal in the long jump and placing fifth in the 100- and 200-meter races.

Alice reflects, "I think what people can learn from John's journey is that there is nothing that you can't do. If you have determination, you can succeed at whatever you put your mind to."

$\mathcal{A}$ FATHER'S JOURNEY

Ever since he was a young boy, Ron Greenfield dreamed of flying.

"My mom told me that from the time I could walk and talk, all I ever talked about was becoming a pilot," says Ron.

Ron's love of aeronautics grew stronger over the years. But it wasn't until he was seventeen that his dream finally came true.

It was 1968, and the Vietnam War was in full swing. Ron enlisted, went through flight school, and began piloting the new Cobra Attack helicopter over the jungles of Vietnam.

"I was flying what we called mortar patrol," explains

Ron. "Mortar patrol is where we keep aircraft up all the time, waiting for either the North Vietnamese Army or the Vietcong to make mortar attacks on the U.S. troops. Once they'd fire the mortar, you could pinpoint it. And then you could quickly roll in, and fire rockets on that spot."

On March 5, 1969, Ron was on a reconnaissance mission when his Cobra was hit by enemy gunfire. The helicopter was badly damaged, and began a steep dive into the jungle below.

"Apparently they hit my flight controls, because I couldn't pull out of the dive," says Ron. "We probably hit the trees at 200 or 250 miles an hour."

"It looked like the jungle just opened up, we went into it, and it closed up," remarks Ron. "You couldn't even tell where we went in."

The Cobra literally came apart in the crash, with only the cockpit remaining intact. Badly injured and bleeding, Ron managed to crawl out of the aircraft, but the excruciating pain made it impossible for him to move any farther. Ultimately, he passed out.

Moments later, Ron's copilot, Terry McDonald, regained consciousness. Dazed and disoriented, Terry staggered toward a clearing in the trees to try to get his bearings. What happened next was a soldier's worst nightmare—the enemy lay in wait, and Terry was captured. Tragically, he would never be heard from again.

Back at the wreckage, however, Ron remained unconscious. In their haste, the enemy soldiers mistakenly left him for dead.

When he finally awoke, hours later, Ron was confused and unsure of where he was. "You know how in the movies, they say, 'Where am I?' That's just how it was." Slowly, he discovered the extent of his injuries. "My flight helmet was shattered, which means I hit my head pretty hard," he comments, "and I felt a real sharp pain in my left leg. I looked down, and the foot was laying flat, even though my leg was straight. When I moved it, the foot flopped all the way over. I could see that half of my boot was gone, that I was bleeding quite a bit. I knew I had to stop this bleeding or I was going to die."

Weak, immobile, and losing more and more blood, Ron knew that it was only a matter of time before he would die or the enemy would return. Summoning up his remaining strength, Ron recalls, "I crawled over to some trees not far from the wreckage. And I put both legs up in the air, against the tree. And that's how I spent the night."

"When I awoke, it was morning. It had been raining, and I remember trying to catch some raindrops with my mouth, 'cause I was thirsty," says Ron. "I began trying to think about how I was gonna get out of there."

The situation seemed hopeless. Three search-and-rescue missions for the two missing pilots had already failed. One helicopter had been shot down, killing three soldiers. A second was badly damaged, and a third was ambushed when it landed.

Unable to walk, Ron had no choice but to wait and pray. He desperately needed a miracle. A few hours later, his prayers were answered when a fourth army helicopter finally spotted him.

"The door gunner had seen a piece of wreckage, and that's what made them turn around," explains Ron. "They sent a medic down on a cable. He hooked me up to a harness, and they hauled me out of there."

The next thing Ron knew, he was waking up in a MASH-unit field hospital. But his ordeal was far from over.

"It was three days before I gained consciousness. And they did emergency surgery on me." Doctors did their best to try and save Ron's leg, but as he tells it, "They told me later they didn't know if I was gonna make it."

Ron was shipped to Japan, where doctors performed additional surgery. But the prognosis wasn't good. Upon his return to the States, Ron would face amputation below the knee.

"I had not realized how seriously I was injured," reveals Ron. "I saw my flying career going away."

When Ron was finally returned home, his doctors felt they could save his leg. But it wouldn't come without a price—the damaged limb had contracted an incurable bone infection, which gave Ron constant pain, and which got progressively worse. "A lot of time was spent on crutches," Ron says.

Four years and sixteen painful surgeries later, Ron had had enough. He was transferred to a military hospital in Denver, Colorado, where, two days later, his foot and lower calf were amputated. The results were immediate and miraculous.

"By 10:00 A.M. I wanted to get out of bed. And they said, 'No, you gotta stay in bed, nobody gets out of bed after an amputation.' I said, 'I feel fine.' The next day I was out of my bed and walking on crutches around the hospital, with absolutely no pain. It was like this huge burden had been lifted," recalls Ron.

Ron's convalescence was amazing. He was fitted with an artificial limb and, as always, he was determined to defy the odds.

"They'd always have to chase me out of therapy," Ron remembers. "I'd get down there and I would spend hours. I was determined I was gonna be a good walker."

Ron became more than just a good walker, however. Soon, he was playing baseball, learning to ski, and running 10K races.

"The attitude I developed," he says, "was that the artificial leg was now a part of me."

Eventually, Ron also came to terms with the fact that his flying career was over. But he was still struggling with one unanswered question.

"I was always asking God, you know, 'Why me? Why did you take my leg?'"

Then in 1992, while on a business trip, Ron came across a newspaper article that helped answer that question. The article described three-year-old Russian twins who'd been born with gangrene in their legs. Both boys had been turned over to an orphanage at infancy—after their legs had been amputated.

"It struck me," Ron says, "that with all I'd been through

over the past couple of decades, I could do something for these two kids that somebody with two good legs couldn't, because I know what they can do and what they can't do.

"I got on the phone to my wife and I pleaded with her that we should adopt these kids," recalls Ron. Next, he contacted the Cradle of Hope, an adoption agency in Washington, D.C., and convinced them that they needed to look no further to place the Russian twins.

"I told everyone that even if it takes more medical care than I thought or if it takes more mental care than I thought, I was gonna bring these boys back and give them an opportunity," declared Ron.

That August, Ron and his wife boarded a plane to Moscow to bring the boys home.

"I went to the orphanage there to see them," remembers Ron, "and they were sitting in a double stroller. And the only way to describe it is that they were even more beautiful than even I expected.

"On the plane back, I looked down at these two little guys as they were sleeping, and it just hit me like a lightning bolt, you know . . . that *that's* the purpose. *That's* the purpose that God had. *That's* why I lost my leg," says Ron. "Because if I hadn't, I probably wouldn't have pursued those two little boys. They wouldn't have jumped out at me like they did."

Ron finally felt that he'd found a reason for all of his suffering. He knew that through his own experience, he could give his sons the confidence to rise above their disabilities.

"They tell me often that they wish they could have real legs," Ron admits. "And when they tell me that, I tell them, well, you know, we're dealt with what we're dealt with, and we just have to make the most of it."

Today the boys, Max and Andy, are fourteen, and they both realize what a special gift their father has given them.

Says Andy, "Dad adopted us because he felt like he can help us. Because, if you have problems, he'll know what to do."

"My dad's my favorite person in the world because he has an artificial leg like I do, and he loves me a lot," adds Max.

That love has made it possible for Max and Andy Greenfield to have the advantage of a full and active life.

"It doesn't keep me from doing what I want to do," says Andy. "I can ride my skateboard, or bike, and sometimes I ride my rollerblades. And I go swimming."

As Ron looks back on his experience, he is awed by the miracles that have touched his life.

"It's been a multitude of miracles," he says. "Surviving the crash, surviving the Vietnamese, and then, I think the final miracle is Andy and Max.

"God put me in the right place at the right time to do another miracle."

PROM NIGHT PROGNOSIS

Like most parents, Karen and John Blod hoped that their daughter Lisa's dreams would come true. They proudly watched as she grew from a happy, carefree child with a love for music and the piano to a young woman preparing to start a life of her own.

"She was getting ready to turn eighteen," says John. "This was her senior year, and before school even started she had already planned out the prom and school activities, and she had wanted it to be that, you know, perfect year in transition to finish out high school."

To help pay for all her senior activities, Lisa took a part-time job at a local restaurant. And it was there on the night of January 26, 2000, that her hopes and dreams began to unravel. Her mother, Karen, had stopped by to see her near the end of her shift.

"She was working and her boyfriend, Joseph, was there waiting for her to get off work. Joseph and Lisa had been going out for two months that night. She asked me if she could go over to Joseph's house later, and I said, 'Well, no, because it's a school night.' Lisa pleaded, 'I know it's late, I know I have midterms, but please. . . .' So I gave in and said, 'Okay, listen, 12:00 A.M., that's it.' Lisa promised, 'Okay, I will be in at five till 12:00 talking to you.' And I said, 'Okay, I'm gonna count on that.' "

But by 12:15 A.M., Lisa had still not returned home.

"I must have dozed off," recalls Karen. "And all of a sudden, the phone rang. I was expecting it to be Lisa, saying, 'Oh, Mom, I'm so sorry that I lost track of time.' But it wasn't her. It was the hospital calling, indicating that she had been in a serious accident. And at that point, my heart just dropped, and I said, 'Oh, my God, is she okay?' "

Karen's worst fear had come true. Lisa's car had crashed head-on into a tree. By the time Karen and John arrived at the hospital, Lisa was in surgery.

"Your stomach is in knots and it's very difficult to even talk to each other," Karen explains. "I think we were so pulled within ourselves, feeling, Oh, my gosh, what are we going to do without her if she doesn't make it? You know, she's our whole life. We just started praying. Praying to God to let her come through this."

After waiting for what seemed like hours, the Blods finally received some news—Lisa was alive, but in a coma.

"One of the first questions I asked the doctor," remembers John, "was, 'Is she gonna make it?' And the doctor said, 'We don't know. If she comes out of the coma in the next three days, everything should be fine, but if it goes beyond three days, there's gonna be complications and problems.'"

Karen adds, "They did indicate that the longer she's under, the worse it can be. She could be paralyzed. She may not walk again, or she may not talk again. She may not be able to feed herself again. I just wanted her to be alive. And then I would work and deal with whatever came after that."

John continues, "The first day she did not come out of the coma. By the time we got to the second day, she still had not come out of it."

As days turned to weeks, Lisa remained comatose. Her boyfriend, Joseph, stayed by her side. Finally, fourteen days after her accident, the Blods received a sign of hope.

"She opened her eyes," explains John. "Just opened them up. And she couldn't move her eyes, but she could open and close her eyelids. And that was the first sign."

But the doctors didn't share the family's optimism.

"At first, the doctor thought it was just a spasm or reaction," John says, "but I told the doctor, 'No, we've been here day in and day out. This is different.' The doctor actually asked Lisa on the second day to blink once for 'yes' and twice for 'no.' Lisa was able to respond 'Yes.'"

Three days later she responded in a new and startling way.

"Lisa began actually making motions with her fingers that at first appeared random," recalls John. "And then, after watching her, I realized she was actually using sign language that she had learned in eighth grade as part of a class project. The doctor came in and indicated that he thought it was just spasms and really did not believe that it was a sign, that he had never heard of such a thing. I told the doctors, 'You don't know Lisa. I know she's signing. I actually did this with her. I know if Lisa wants to communicate, she's gonna find a way, and this is her way. She's trying to get through to us.'"

It wasn't long before Lisa was sitting up, still unable to speak, but communicating with her father through a sign language chart.

"The first letters that I could recognize," John remembers with wonder, "were D–A–D . . . 'Dad.' I was very excited, very excited that she was communicating. I was very excited that she knew who I was."

Lisa had emerged from the coma. But according to Dr. Kimberly Bedell, who was in charge of her rehabilitation, she still had a very long way to go.

"When Lisa started her pediatric rehabilitation," explains Dr. Bedell, "she did not speak. She was using some crude sign language to communicate basic needs. She wasn't able to move her legs much. And so at that point, she was quite dependent on everyone for her care."

But Lisa was determined to get by on her own, and she

had a special goal—to attend her senior prom, which was four weeks away.

"The doctors said she's gonna be lucky to make it to her June graduation, let alone an April prom," recalls Karen. "And I said that she really wants to go to this. She needs to go to this. This is her senior prom. That's not ever going to happen again."

Dr. Bedell continued Lisa's rehabilitation as she slowly learned to walk again.

"The day they actually put her on the parallel bars to take a step or two," Karen says, "she took three steps. And I was just almost in tears. I mean, I literally had to go outside, get on my cell phone, and call my husband at work and say, 'She walked! She walked today!' The next day at therapy, she walked the full length of the parallel bars and back. It was just amazing to me. I couldn't believe it. I knew all along that she was determined, but she became more determined as she progressed."

Dr. Bedell agrees, "I think we were all kind of doubtful that she would be walking out of the hospital a week early. And it ends up that it was actually two weeks early. That was remarkable."

"Nobody expected it to come true," adds Lisa. "I knew it would, but nobody else really thought that I was serious or that it could happen."

And Lisa's dream to attend her senior prom came true, thanks to her courage and determination.

"That determination and that strength had to come from somewhere," Lisa says, "and I believe that it was a miracle that I had that determination and that strength."

"The miracle," says John, "was Lisa coming out of this coma and coming back one hundred percent and getting her life back, which the doctors said wouldn't happen."

"I go over it and over it in my head," agrees Lisa, "and there is no reason why I should be sitting here talking right now. And so, it's got to be a miracle."

BLIND AMBITION

In early 1993, Lisa Fittipaldi was the picture of success. She had a loving husband, a thriving career, and a very busy schedule.

"At the time," says Lisa, "I was working forty or fifty hours a week as a professional, and driving to work, and going grocery shopping, and doing the normal things that we all do."

And then, in March, Lisa's life was suddenly thrown out of focus.

"I was driving down I-35," Lisa recounts, "and there was a semi in front of me, and all of a sudden, the semi disappeared."

For one terrifying moment, Lisa went completely blind. She dismissed the incident, but a few weeks later, it happened again. Deeply shaken, she called her husband, Al.

"She explained the situation to me," recalls Al, "that she was driving, and all of a sudden her vision just blacked out, and she almost hit a truck."

Lisa refused to get back behind the wheel, and during the next month, the episodes became more frequent.

"I thought I was having a brain aneurysm, because one minute I would see something, and the next minute I wouldn't see it," Lisa says. "Then the colors would start fading away, and everything became a milky color, like it had a handkerchief over it."

But her doctors could not pinpoint the exact cause of the problem.

Dr. Michael Nacol explains, "Initially, when she was seen by her eye doctor, she started out with a corneal irregularity that made her vision distorted. Not only did she have hazy vision but her vision field was decreased."

Lisa underwent several surgeries to cure her condition, but her eyesight continued to deteriorate. And slowly, her world disappeared into complete darkness.

"It was like a grey-black obscurity," describes Lisa. "Even talking about it makes my stomach go into knots. It is incredibly hard to even describe the kind of panic you have."

Lisa was eventually diagnosed with a rare form of vasculitis, a disease that was attacking the nerves in her eyes, and that would leave her legally and permanently blind.

"The first thought I had was," says Lisa, "my life is

over. Simple as that. You can't see, what can you possibly do? Seventy percent of everything you do is done with your eyes first, whether you notice it or not."

"She broke down into tears," Al remembers, "and pretty much knew that in a very short period of time, her world as she knew it was gonna go away. And that's a hard thing to take."

Lisa tried desperately to adjust to a life in the shadows. But even the simplest activities had become an enormous challenge.

"After a while," admits Lisa, "you feel like it's just not worth the effort. The world is dark, let's just stay in the bedroom because the space is comfortable, and you know where you are, and why move?"

Adds Al, "She didn't want to have to fend for herself. It was like, hang up a towel for me, or get me this, or get me that. I think I started getting a little angry at having to do for her when I knew she could care for herself."

And then, in May of 1995, Lisa received a phone call from a friend asking her to join her at a two-week painting seminar in Louisiana.

"She said, 'There's a man out there, and he's supposed to be very motivational,'" recalls Lisa. "'And you just sleep in a dormitory and you get away from Al, 'cause you've been with him day and night now for a year.' And I said, Okay, I can do this."

"The friend never showed up," Al continues. "So Lisa, rather than canceling the class, wound up saying, 'Would you drive me to Louisiana?'"

Lisa attended the seminar on her own, and the two

weeks away helped boost her confidence. Although some of her classmates expressed skepticism about a blind person's ability to paint, Lisa became determined to prove them wrong.

"I said, Well, why not?" recounts Lisa. "Why can't I do this? If I learned how to get dressed again, and I learned how to eat with a knife and fork again, why can't I paint?"

"Can darks be luminous, bright, and powerful all at the same time? Yes," says Al.

With Al's help, Lisa began absorbing everything there was to know about painting.

"We went through hundreds of volumes of art books, magazines, catalogs," Al says.

"That's when I realized how difficult it was to paint if you can't see what you're doing," explains Lisa. "You can't verify in front of you what you've painted. And that's when I started to teach myself how to *feel* if a paint pigment and watercolor was yellow, versus blue, versus red."

Once Lisa memorized the various color formulas, she perfected a technique called "mental mapping," which helped her find where she was on the canvas. Soon, Lisa was creating beautiful life scenes in intricate detail. And before long, she was displaying and selling her work at art fairs around the country. Lisa's mysterious ability shocked everyone, including her close friend, Claudia Lane.

"I couldn't fathom how she could paint with such depth and detail," says Claudia. "I couldn't even speak. I didn't know what to say at that point because it was so amazing. It was like watching a miracle."

In the summer of 1999, Lisa caught the attention of Jason Siegel, a gallery owner from Austin, Texas.

"One day I received a packet in the mail," recalls Jason. "I get packets from artists asking me to review their work and consider representing them. And I was very intrigued with the work, you know, very intrigued that she was blind and that she could paint realism."

Jason arranged to meet Lisa for lunch and quickly agreed to represent her. The very next day, he sold one of her paintings.

"When I would show people these paintings," says Jason, "I'd say, 'What do you think of this painting?' And they'd say, 'Oh, that's a beautiful painting. I really like it.' And I'd say, 'Well, what would you say if I told you this artist happens to be blind?' And they'd just be blown away by that and want to know the rest of the story."

Seven years after her odyssey began, Lisa has become a full-time artist, painting seven hours a day, seven days a week in her studio, "Blind Ambition," and selling her work through one of the largest galleries in the country. Her incredible transformation amazes even those closest to her.

"It blows you away," Jason says, "that somebody who can't even see can paint these most amazing paintings, and get these compositions, and balance—all these things other artists are trying to achieve in their paintings."

"How she does this is a miracle," adds Claudia. "She sketches it out in pencil. She puts the color on and she gets this incredible piece of art that is totally unexplainable."

Al agrees, "I'm not really sure there is an explanation as

to how someone is given a gift. What Lisa has given to me, and what I know she has given to others, is hope for the future. A feeling that life is wonderful and that you should live every moment to the fullest because you never know what's going to happen."

"I'm just very fortunate," concludes Lisa. "There's always been an angel on my shoulder—or a leprechaun, probably, knowing me. One day I would like to be noted as a good painter, a good artist. That's what I'm striving for."

BACK ON TRACK

Ever since he was a young boy, Kent Desormeaux dreamed of becoming a jockey, regardless of the dangers involved.

Sonia Desormeaux, Kent's wife, says, "Being a jockey's wife is very stressful. The danger of his work is just something that you can't get used to. Every race you just sit and hope that he comes back okay."

"This young man is an athlete of the highest caliber, and he was winning many, many races," says announcer Gary Henson. "At the beginning of December 1992, Kent was well on his way to becoming the leading moneys-earned-in-a-year jockey in the entire history of horse racing. And this, I'm sure, was his target goal as he was riding early on in the meet at Hollywood Park."

"Kent was having a wonderful year," agrees Sonia. "And we were also expecting the birth of our first child."

"December 11, 1992, started out as just another average racing day," recalls fellow jockey Corey Black. "Nothing in particular early in the day told me...gave me signs of what was to come. And it's a day I'll definitely never forget."

"It was rainy. The track was listed as fast, but it was wet and quickly getting muddy," remembers Joy Scott, another of Kent's colleagues.

The horse Kent was riding that day was Judge Hammer, number eleven.

"It was a good break, it was clean, the horses were running well. Judge Hammer was the favorite in that race because of his past performances that showed he looked like he was going to win," says Gary.

"The horse I was riding was Cartagena Slew. He has one run, one strong run; he'll give you everything he has," says Joy. "My instructions were to save it for the stretch."

"Now, rounding the far turn is where the race really begins," explains Gary, "and Kent took his horse to the outside coming-down lane. There were four horses right across the track. And then Judge Hammer kind of came between those as they spread out, and took command as they were coming down the lane."

Coming to the wire, Kent gave the horse two cracks with the whip. Suddenly, it veered across the track and into the path of Joy Scott's horse.

"When I hit him, it was...it was shocking," remembers Joy. "I had saved my horse for the finish, and in the stretch drive he was giving me everything. And I looked up and I see the eleven horse loose on the outside.

"You see a loose horse, you look for a rider," says Joy. "But it happened to be right in front of me, and it was too late. The impact was incredible, and it scared me to death. I felt sick to my stomach."

"When I returned to the jockeys' quarters, I felt like I should call his wife to let her know what had happened," says Corey.

"My initial feeling when I heard about Kent's accident was, Is it going to be this time when he's really hurt bad?" Sonia says. "And it was. He almost died the first night. They couldn't get his brain to stop bleeding. There was too much swelling and they didn't think he would make it."

The stress and the worry caused Sonia to go into premature labor, but Kent astounded his doctors with a miraculous recovery.

"Even with all of the injuries he had, he managed to get out of the hospital and be there for our child's birth," says Sonia fondly.

"Can you imagine, being all broke up, can't go to work, but you get the most wonderful Christmas present in the whole world?" declares Kent.

But thinking back on his accident, Kent says, "I get chills. I have chills right now thinking about it.

"December was, mentally, a roller-coaster ride for me. I had, like, seven or eight fractures that bled everywhere.

But the main fractures, they went all the way across my head this way and that way," describes Kent. "I was out for six weeks, deeply concerned about when in the world I was going to be able to ride again."

"When Kent was rehabilitating, I definitely had some doubts about him ever coming back, mostly because of the equilibrium problem," recalls Corey.

"I got dizzy on occasions," admits Kent. "You know, if I would stick my head down between my legs and then stand up real fast, I was dizzy. And I wasn't about to play around with horses until I could do that."

In the meantime, Kent used a mechanical horse called the "Equicizer," which duplicates the rhythm and pace of a running horse.

"It has a bridle on it, you know, it even looks exactly like a horse's head and everything, and I can sit up there and ride," says Kent. "So, actually, what I would do is, I would watch the replays at night and I would ride nine races. When the field would turn for home on TV, I'd start riding the Equicizer. It was what I used to rehabilitate. I wanted to prove that I could do it again. Can I be number one again, you know? Can I?"

And several weeks later, he had his chance.

"On the day that I rode my first horse back, Shrewd Vixen, I can still see the bars of the gate in front of me, and I'm thinking, Am I gonna fall? Am I ready? What are these people gonna think?" recalls Kent. "I have to perform like I've never performed before. But that adrenaline pump you get, about the idea that you might win, that's what makes you forget about the fears of what might happen. As the doors opened, I swear, for about thirty yards I was completely lost.

"The first thing I did was cut the corner, split the horses, you know, went through every tight spot I could, whether it was a right or wrong decision, just to prove I wasn't scared," Kent says.

"This guy was almost dead," declares Gary, "and he came back, and he won his very first race. That shows you what kind of champion athlete this guy is."

They say that if you take a fall, you should get right back on the horse—but no one watching Kent Desormeaux's tragic accident that day expected him to live, let alone come back as a winner. It's a miracle that thrilled both his fans and the young jockey himself.

"I just wanted to shout in the air, and go crazy," Kent recalls. "It was a wild feeling. Desormeaux's back!"

ALL GOD'S CREATURES

BORIS AND THE BIG APPLE

In 1996, Barbara Listenik was living in Fort Lauderdale, Florida, with her constant companion Boris, a beautiful mixed-breed boxer.

"I got Boris when he was two years old. He's the most lovable dog in the whole wide world. He knows when I'm happy. He knows when I'm sad. He's a very big part of my life. I don't have children and I'm not married, so he's like my child. He's my best friend," Barbara says.

Just before Christmas, Barbara made arrangements to move to Brooklyn, New York. She was renting a moving van, but decided to send Boris via airfreight to spare him the long drive.

"Boris had never flown before, so I was very worried for him. I did everything that I thought was necessary to get him there safely. I did everything the airline recommended as well."

That included removing Boris's identification collar so it wouldn't get snagged during the flight. Barbara gave Boris one last hug and lured him into the crate with his favorite toy bunny. She was worried for her best friend's comfort but excited to start her new life with him in Brooklyn.

"My thoughts when Boris was in the air were, Please, please, let him get there safely."

But when she arrived at LaGuardia Airport to pick him up, her fears became reality.

"The airport staff took me in back and they said, 'Miss, there's a little bit of a problem. There was an accident.' Then the supervisor walks up to a bloody, crunched-up, empty carrier. I knew that they must have dropped him or driven something into him. And my immediate thought was, Oh, my God, is he alive or dead?"

The supervisor told her that Boris had been seen running around on the tarmac and that they had their cargo crew personnel chasing him right then.

"Well," said Barbara, "he's going to keep running. You're never going to get him. He's scared to death. Just let me go out there—one whistle and he'll come running to me."

The supervisor insisted that they had the situation under control. And for the next two hours, Barbara waited anxiously for some word of her injured dog. When the supervisor finally came back out, he had bad news—Boris had evaded the cargo crew and crossed the fence from the tarmac onto the highway. He had last been seen running over the overpass into Corona, Queens.

"You idiots!" screamed Barbara. She ran from the airport in tears and jumped in the car. Alone and heartbroken in a strange city, she drove in circles, searching for Boris. He was lost somewhere off the eastern edge of Manhattan and if Barbara didn't locate him quickly, he could end up anywhere in New York City.

"Boris had never been in the noisy streets. He'd never been in New York City. It was like looking for a needle in a haystack. At first I was looking for his body, and then some kid said he saw this dog that was tan-and-white, running like a bullet. That gave me hope. I said to myself, He's alive. He's alive."

Alive but lost in one of the largest cities in the world.

"I searched all night in the rain and the cold, just walking up and down the streets, calling his name. And on Christmas Eve, I really realized how impossible the situation was. Here I was, this tiny little speck of dust in this big city looking for a lost dog. I've never felt so alone in my entire life. I didn't know what to do. I just kept calling for him, 'Boris, I know you're out there. Please come home.'"

On Christmas morning, Barbara returned to the airport.

"I went to the supervisor and said, 'Okay, we have a situation. What are we gonna do about this? You lost my dog.' And the supervisor says, 'Yes, miss, I'm filling out the form now.' And he just reached under the desk and pulled out a baggage-claim form and said, 'This is all we can do.' 'This is a baggage-claim form,' I said. 'Are you telling me my dog is baggage?' I almost collapsed. My dog is considered baggage! I never knew in a million years that animals were considered luggage, and that the law hasn't been changed since 1929. I said, 'This is the most ridiculous thing I've ever heard in my entire life! My dog is not a piece of luggage. He's my baby. He's like my child.' "

The supervisor just shrugged and apologized again. Immediately, Barbara ran home and went through her boxes, still unpacked, to find pictures of Boris. She pulled out her fax machine and started running off flyers. She spent the rest of Christmas Day putting up missing-dog posters throughout Corona, Queens.

That night, Barbara returned home even more exhausted and depressed. How could she possibly celebrate under the circumstances? Wiping away tears, she started decorating her tree. She swore to herself, I am not going to light this tree until he's found. And I'm going to keep this tree until he sits next to it with me.

Barbara realized that the job was too big for just one person, so she tried a different approach.

"I asked myself what the best way was to get the word out that Boris was lost, and I said, Okay, let me call the newspaper."

She found a sympathetic ear in *New York Post* reporter Laura Italiano, who found herself unexpectedly touched by Barbara's story.

"Barbara called the *New York Post* absolutely frantic. Typically, we're busy chasing murderers, political corruption. It took a special kind of story to get us to care about a little lost dog. And Barbara was the one who made that happen for us. The *Post* absolutely loved the story. It is a classic tabloid story. You have a clear-cut villain, this bungling airline, and a very sympathetic victim—a poor dog who had been lost. I think everyone's heart went out to Barbara. This is a woman who doesn't know New York City, knew no one in town, and she had this tremendous responsibility to find an animal in completely unfamiliar surroundings. You had to feel for her; you had to worry about her," Laura says.

"I couldn't believe how many people responded," Barbara marveled. "It touched so many people's hearts."

One of those hearts belonged to Paula Forester, a professional psychic who saw Boris's picture on a television news program. Paula was amazed at her reaction to the picture. "They did a close-up on his eyes, and *pow*. There was a psychic connection. I have worked psychically with animals before, but I have never felt such a strong and urgent connection to anything before that point."

Paula immediately contacted Barbara.

"She told me that she was a psychic and that she was getting strong feelings from Boris. They were communicating. My first reaction was, Hey, lady, if you're communicating with my dog, tell him to come home! She told me that she didn't want a reward, she didn't want pay, she just wanted to get Boris back to me. I didn't believe in that hocus-pocus-type stuff, but I just wanted my baby home. I wasn't going to turn away anyone volunteering to help find him."

Paula turned out to be more than just a volunteer. She was a force to be reckoned with.

"She was pushing me, and I thought I was the aggressive one. She told me, 'Come on, let's go, you can do it, you can do it. Keep going, keep going.' She was really doing the legwork, really going out there getting the flyers out."

"I knew Boris was alive," Paula said. "And I knew he was desperate to find Barbara again. He was very confused and very, very sad. Every time I linked in psychically to Boris, the sadness, confusion, and heartache were overwhelming."

"We went from neighborhood to neighborhood. We just kept looking every night, in the cold. We just never stopped," Barbara said.

"What really kept me going was this little dog that had a really big psychic voice that said, 'Please help me,'" Paula said.

But after days of searching, Barbara's hopes began to fade.

Barbara remembered, "New Year's had come and gone, and it was so cold. With the wind-chill factor it was 25 below zero outside. All I could do was cry. I couldn't imagine how Boris was surviving."

Meanwhile, Barbara's friends and family were worried sick about her and urged her to accept reality and get on with her life. But Barbara wouldn't give up.

"Some people told me, 'Oh, it's only a dog,'" Barbara recalled. "You know, get over it, get another one. And I told them, 'You don't understand. There is no closure. I can't live my life knowing that he's out there, he's cold, he's hungry, he's starving.' I said, 'I'm not gonna give up on him.'"

And the media was standing by Barbara's decision.

Laura Italiano says, "We started running a story a week in the *Post,* and Barbara kept us well-fed with updates. She felt that if the newspaper kept up a steady drumbeat to search for this dog, that public attention wouldn't just die down. And he wouldn't die out there, unmourned, unsearched for."

But all the publicity only produced more false leads. The phone rang around the clock with sightings of strays from people anxious to help, but all turned out to be dead ends. Barbara was completely physically and emotionally exhausted. She didn't know how much longer she could continue.

Luckily, she had Paula Forester to help keep her spirits up. "Her energy just kept me going," she said, "and really it was a godsend that she did come along."

Paula said, "The worst thing you can do is get discouraged. I just knew he was out there. I told Barbara not to give up. I don't care if it takes two months; I don't care if it takes three months. The dog is coming home. Alive."

Several weeks later, despite all of Laura Italiano's best efforts, the publicity and the media attention hadn't produced a single solid lead. But a strange recurring dream was about to change the parameters of the search.

Paula tossed and turned for hours every night, dreaming of Boris. She said, "I would get images of Boris sleeping in tires, of him having a bloody foot, starving and very cold. I knew that I was picking up what the dog was feeling. Boris was freezing and desperate."

The dream eventually led Paula to an automotive shop in Queens.

"I must have driven by this one auto repair place a hundred times. I actually went up and approached one of the workers there, asking about a stray. The man was so busy, he really kind of brushed me off."

It seemed like just another dead end. Unfortunately, at this point, the media was also beginning to question its involvement in the search. Even the indomitable Laura was giving up hope. "Maybe we were doing the wrong thing keeping this story going, because the more time that passed, the less likely it was that there would be a happy ending."

Barbara had to make a tough decision. "I didn't know whether to keep going on with this endless search or get on with my life. It was really getting to the point where reality started checking in with me. But Paula said to me, 'Barbara, if you give up, this dog's going to give up and die. The only reason he's staying alive is because he knows you're out there looking for him.'"

After weeks and weeks of searching, Paula received a tip on yet another sighting of Boris. Paula received a call at her apartment from a stranger in Queens, a man who said, "I think I have the dog that's in the flyer. There's been a stray dog living in this garbage-filled abandoned lot next to my house. And sometimes we throw leftovers over the fence because we feel sorry for him. It kind of looks like the dog in the picture."

The call brought Paula back to a familiar location. The man's apartment was next door to the automotive shop she'd visited days before. The man had brought the dog into the apartment. Paula stood in his apartment, looked at the dog, looked at the picture, then looked at the dog again. "His eyes were soulless, they were dead. He was filthy. He was a different color. He had a slash in his foot, almost all the way through. I walked up to him and said, 'Boris, is that you?' And then one ear went up and one ear went down. And I said, Oh, my God. It's Boris after fifty-two days."

Her hands shaking, Paula immediately called Barbara. "Barbara," she said, "we have Boris."

"I can't go and look at any more dogs," Barbara answered. "Are you sure it's him? I'm so tired. I don't know how much more I can take. Are you sure?"

"Somebody called me. He's inside a house. This is definitely your dog. You gotta come here now."

"Paula, I can't go through this anymore," Barbara said. She didn't have an ounce of strength left.

"Look, I'm telling you. One ear up, one ear down. You've gotta come down here. He's only a mile from the airport."

"I'm on my way."

Weeks of sorrow and worry were about to come to an

end. "I went inside this apartment complex and there he was, this little dog coming around the corner peeking its head out at me. And I looked and I said, 'That's not my dog. Boris has beautiful eyes. He's got a tan coat. This dog's skinny.'"

"Barbara, please," Paula begged. "Just look again."

Barbara kneeled down and looked the limping, bedraggled dog in the eye. "Boris," she called softly, "Boris, is that you?" And he looked up at her with one ear up and one ear down, and suddenly Barbara let out a yell. "Oh, my God, Boris, it *is* you! It's you!" She was shaking all over, and suddenly her legs gave out. She found herself sitting on the floor with Boris licking her face, crying. Everyone else in the room was crying right along with her.

"I missed you so much," Barbara told Boris tearfully. "I love you. I can't believe they found you!"

"It was the most beautiful thing," Paula remembered. "It was worth every minute of whatever I contributed as a part of this bigger picture. It was the best reward and the most miraculous. And it was a miracle. It was a chance in a billion."

That night, Barbara kept her promise. After weeks of waiting, her Christmas tree was finally lit to welcome Boris home. "We'll make it all better," she told Boris. "Look at the pretty tree with the lights. You're home. You're home, baby!"

The next morning, a triumphant *New York Post* headline greeted all of New York City. And Boris immediately became a media darling.

A reporter said, "After six weeks of street life, the boxer was finally home. He's a trooper. He held in there. I can't believe it. All the while his owner kept faith. But it was a little magic that brought him home."

And Paula Forester helped provide some of that magic. She and Barbara continue to be close friends, and today Barbara is far less skeptical of psychic phenomena.

"Our chances psychically or otherwise were one in a billion," Paula says. "I could have been totally wrong through this whole thing. It was a miracle that Boris was found."

"I'm a believer," Barbara says. "There are some powers out there that you can't dismiss. To find a lost dog in New York City? Anything could have happened to him. Anything. For me to be reunited with him is a total miracle to me."

RUPERT, THE PARROT

Lynn Norley of Bryn Mawr, Pennsylvania, has a very special relationship with Rupert, her African Gray Parrot.

"There's definitely something magical about this bird," she says. "I mean, the bird just interacts with everyone in such a way that's so touching. His affection, and his rapport, and how he absolutely knows what's going on around him—it's just fantastic."

Lynn acquired Rupert as a baby in 1986, and since then, the parrot has become a central part of her life. In fact, she literally wouldn't be alive today if it weren't for Rupert.

It all began in February of 1998, when Lynn put Rupert in his cage for the night, and went to bed herself.

What she didn't know was that in just a few hours she would wake to a living nightmare.

"I was lying there and I heard a very loud thud. Rupert fell off his perch, and then I heard him squawking very loudly. It was definitely an alarm sound. I mean, there wasn't any doubt in my mind that there was a problem," she remembers.

Lynn went to investigate, but got no farther than the bedroom door, which opened to reveal smoke and flames. "I was faced with a wall of smoke that was horrible-smelling, and I couldn't see anything."

She knew that Rupert was in danger. Not thinking of the consequences, she rushed to free him from his cage as the room filled with smoke.

"When I got to the cage, I was extremely panicked, and I was sure that Rupert wouldn't make it. This parrot can take only a little bit of smoke. I couldn't find the door of the cage because I couldn't see, and I couldn't get a breath, either. But somehow I fumbled and found the cage, and I grabbed Rupert out from the bottom."

With Rupert tucked under her arm, Lynn rushed out to her patio for air. She took a deep breath, and ran back into the smoke-filled house to rescue her dogs, Alex and Panther, who were still trapped in the fire. The dogs were frantic, and in the middle of all the chaos, Lynn felt Rupert go lifeless in her arms.

"I was sure that Rupert had died," says Lynn. "I felt horrible, because Rupert was such a part of my life for so long, and I couldn't just drop him on the floor." With the fire burning around her, Lynn didn't have a lot of time to make a decision. "I wrapped Rupert in a bathrobe, and gave him the only burial I could at the moment. I put him in the bottom of the shower stall."

Lynn could hear the flames crackling in the hallway outside the door. She put a wet shirt over her face, grabbed her dogs, and tried to make a run for it.

"I put Alex under my arm and grabbed Panther by the collar. I planned on going out the bedroom door, but when I opened the door again, I was hit with a wall of smoke and an explosion. I realized then that the house was bursting into flames, and I knew I had to escape through one of the windows of my second-story bedroom."

Thankfully, Lynn and the dogs dropped safely to the ground, leaving the house in flames. Firefighters doused the fire, but only after the inside had been totally gutted.

"It was terrifying, and it was horrible. I was watching my house exploding and smoke coming out of the roof," remembers Lynn.

The next morning, with the support of friends, Lynn returned home to see the devastation the fire had caused. The building was still standing, but it was merely a shell. There was little left in its charred interior. For Lynn, however, the greatest loss was Rupert.

"It seemed that nothing in the house could possibly survive," she says. "The windows were all blown out. In order to fight the fire, the firefighters had thrown everything out the window—my grandmother's things, and my paintings, and all that—but they really didn't matter. I mean, really, truly, the only thing I felt bad about was the bird."

Lynn didn't have the heart to go into the bathroom, so her friend Laurie Moore went in to remove the dead bird. Blackened debris had filled the shower stall after firefighters had doused the blaze, and Laurie pulled away the remains of crumbled walls.

"I started rummaging through the tile and the plaster and the fiberglass," Laurie recalls. "I moved some of it away, and found Rupert plastered up in the corner, looking at me. 'Rupert!' I screamed. Both of us were very surprised, looking at each other, and when I reached down to pick him up, he bit me." Laurie yelled out to Lynn to come quickly, that Rupert was alive.

"When I heard her scream, I couldn't believe my ears," says Lynn. "I ran into the bathroom, and there was Rupert, sitting in the corner of the shower stall on top of a pile of debris. He was shaking, and looked horrible." But finding the bird living, Lynn declares, "It was really a miracle.... No one could believe the bird was alive."

Today, Lynn and Rupert are living happily together in a new home. Lynn owes her life to her pet bird. It was Rupert's warning calls that saved her from the fire. But what saved Rupert?

"I don't know how the bird's alive," Lynn reflects. "It's a miracle that this bird lived through that. I mean, it's totally astounding. Between everything that Rupert inhaled, and everything that happened to him...if even a small part of any of those things had happened to any other bird, it would never have had a chance to live. And everything that happened to Rupert was so intense. It was just really a miracle."

DOG ANGEL

In 1993, John and Toni Sheridan shared their home in rural Virginia with a very special companion, a dog named Sailor who had been a member of the family for more than a decade.

Toni says, "I guess I loved Sailor so much because we really got him as a little pup. He was just five weeks old. We brought him up, we nourished him, and he was just closer to us than a baby."

Sailor may have been Toni's baby, but he was John's best friend.

"Every time I hopped into my pickup to go somewhere," John explains, "he'd be right there alongside me with his head on my knee."

And then, returning from a drive one morning, Sailor waited a moment before his normal routine of jumping out the passenger side of the truck. But this time, something went wrong.

John remembers, "He hit the ground, and he let out a yip, and he just laid there. So I figured, well, in a few minutes he'll get up and walk around, but he just laid there the way he hit the ground. And I knew darn well something had happened. He was paralyzed."

John and Toni rushed Sailor to the local vet.

Toni continues, "The vet said he was hurt internally, and, you know, there was very little he could do. And he suggested putting him to sleep, and there's no way we wanted that. We wanted to keep him and see what would happen."

"So we took him home," says John. "We put him in the bedroom there and made a nice bed for him and he just laid there. I tried to give him some water and he wouldn't drink. I tried to give him some food and he wouldn't eat. After two days or so, he got steadily worse. His eyes were closed half the time and I told Toni, 'He's paralyzed. He can't move. So . . . I think tomorrow morning when the vet opens up, we'll have to take Sailor there and put him to sleep.'"

But Toni refused to give up hope. She told John, " 'I'm going to go and say a prayer. I'm going to ask God to send us an angel.' I prayed and I prayed and I prayed for him."

But Sailor wasn't getting any better. And it was killing John to watch his faithful friend suffer.

"So I looked at Sailor, and I said, 'Well, I guess you know it's the end.' So I slipped off his collar, and I went out to the shed. I had a couple of dog collars from previous dogs I had, and I hung Sailor's collar next to them. It was something I hated to do, but it brought tears to my eyes. Those three collars represented almost forty years of faithful companionship."

The next morning, John was up an hour before taking Sailor to the vet. And that's when something entirely unexpected happened.

John recounts, "I looked up and I saw this little brown dog coming down the driveway. She looked lost. And I looked, but there was no collar on the dog. So I said, Well, heck, she must be hungry. I took her in the house, but she wouldn't eat anything. She started walking around the house. She walked into the bedroom where Sailor was, and she sat down right in front of Sailor, just looking at him. After a minute or so, she went up and she nudged Sailor. And believe it or not, he slowly tried to get to his feet. He was shaky as all heck. He got up and he walked to the door, and that little dog went out, and Sailor followed her out. I couldn't believe it, that Sailor was almost ready to be put to sleep, and here he was walking around wagging his tail and all.

"So I called Toni, and she came out and she said, 'Oh, my God, Sailor's alive! God must have sent an angel.'"

Toni agrees. "Something happened. I don't know what kind of angel He sent, but He sent something to get Sailor up and moving and following that little dog the way he was, and I was just overjoyed."

But there was still the question of this stray dog. Where

had it come from? And was some anxious owner desperately searching for it? John called the local radio station to report a lost dog. A few hours later, the dog's owner called to retrieve her pet. Her name was Karen Jarett.

John explains, "She had just moved up recently from Atlanta, Georgia. They lived three or four miles away, with a big wooded section between us. The dog didn't know this area, and ran into the woods and never came back. Something brought that dog through those woods right to my house, and right to Sailor. And in my opinion, that dog saved Sailor's life."

As the owner thanked John for saving her dog, she pulled a collar from her bag. And at that moment, John understood what had happened.

"She had a collar in her hand, and she put it on the dog," John says. "And I looked at the collar and I called Toni. There was 'Angel' written on the name tag. Toni saw it, and she said, 'That's God's angel.'"

Toni says, "I thanked God because I knew it was through Him that this happened with Sailor. And I knew that if it wasn't for Him, this miracle would never have happened, because to me it was a miracle."

John wonders, "How could a dog come through three or four miles of woods in a strange place? And come right up, nudge my dog, and bring him back to life? This is something that happened without any help from mankind. Something stronger than a human being saved Sailor.

"And it was that little dog."

ILVERBACK SAVIOR

Visiting the wild animals at the local zoo on the Isle of Jersey in Great Britain seemed like a perfect Sunday outing for Brian Lelion and his family.

"I suppose we were only there about five or six minutes before we moved over to the gorilla complex," remembers Brian. "Just as I was getting there, I heard a woman in distress who was screaming, 'My baby, my baby!'"

Five-year-old Levan Merritt had fallen over the wall into the gorilla pit, as his father, Stephen, watched in horror.

"And I saw all of this, this blood from the back of Levan's head, and I didn't think, you know, that we were going to get him out alive," says Stephen.

Meanwhile, Brian Lelion recalls, "I was videotaping this one gorilla, and I knew he was going to come down, to walk over to the little boy that was unconscious on the ground. My first reaction was that the gorilla was going to do something terrible perhaps. He was just getting closer and closer." Brian says, "I don't think anybody knew what to do, because nobody could jump over the wall and go down there. It was such a height. Everything seemed to happen very slowly.

"It was really a shock to see that this massive animal was leaning over this little boy," he remarks.

"I just couldn't believe what I was seeing," says Stephen. "Everybody was in a panic. They were asking where the keepers were, to get someone to help him to get the child out."

Levan's mother wasn't even allowed to look. "They knew that I was his mother, so they wouldn't actually let me look over the wall. They took me 'round the back, and made me cups of tea," she says.

Stephen, however, watched in horror as the giant gorilla approached his son. But then he noticed something else. "This big one seemed to be protecting him, seemed to be keeping the littler ones away," he realized.

"I was surprised that the gorilla just sat there, and just looked up at the people," says Brian Lelion, "so obviously he was really interested and quite tame, really, toward the boy. The gorilla stroked him, and sniffed him, and pulled up his shirt with his finger to get the boy's scent."

"It was a surprise that the gorillas seemed to be gentler

than you'd expect," agrees Stephen. "You'd think they'd have gone and tried to tear someone to pieces."

Moments later, little Levan regained consciousness and discovered the frightening circumstances he was in. His terrified cries scared the older gorilla away.

"I heard him cry, so I managed to look over the wall," says Levan's mother. "When I looked over the wall, he had turned onto his back. And all I could see was just this mass of blood. It was just awful."

When Levan started screaming, Stephen explains, "The big gorilla just wanted to get out of the way, and he went inside the main gorilla enclosure." Zookeeper Andy Wood could hear the young boy's cries as he tried to lure the other gorillas inside.

"During the process of bringing the silverback in, and the adult females, a young male got shut outside," recounts Andy. "It was unavoidable, unfortunately, but at least we ended up with only one animal in the outside area." Recalling his entrance into the gorilla pit, Andy says, "When I first entered the gorilla pit, I took a short stick with me as just a deterrent, perhaps to put the young male off from charging. I asked another zookeeper to come into the enclosure to assist me, in case he got past me. I approached the child, who was semiconscious, with blood around his ears. He'd obviously taken a very hard hit to the head."

Paramedic Brian Fox was the next to jump into the fray.

"There was blood coming out of his mouth and his

ear," Brian Fox remembers. "While he's on his side and screaming, you've got time. But as soon as he went onto his back, you've run out of time. Then there is an immediate danger, because he could choke on his own vomit or blood.

"But once I got him onto his side, I was happy with that situation," says Brian Fox. "I've got one eye on Levan, and the other eye on this gorilla running around." The young gorilla, Brian says, would "run in at times, just to show that he's boss, and to make a noise, and then run off."

"The young male was excitable, ran up and down, and charging a bit," agrees Andy. "In a situation like that, where you've got an excitable gorilla, you perhaps have to be a little more bold than you would be normally." In the gorilla's defense, Andy emphasizes, "He's a very outgoing gorilla, I mean, very playful, very boisterous. That's his personality. Basically, he appears very, very aggressive, but most of it isn't. A lot of it's bluff."

However, Brian Fox says, "With the gorilla running around, you couldn't go to the doors, which are right across the other side of the complex. The only way out quickly—and we had to be quick—was to come up on the rope that they lowered down to me. And then thirty or forty people just pulled me straight up the wall."

"I think this is probably the worst thing a parent can go through," declares Stephen. "I actually thought, I'd raised the child to five years old, and that was it. That that was the end of his life."

"There was a big cheer when the boy came up," says Brian Fox. "And then they put him into the ambulance, and rushed him to the hospital."

"The ambulance man was paler than anybody I'd ever seen in my life," adds Andy. "He was just drained."

"Levan was in the hospital for three weeks," his mother says. "He's had a very severe skull fracture, and he's got to be careful with his arm. But apart from that, he's just like any normal child of his age."

"First time I saw the video was in hospital, and I was on the news," recalls Levan. "When I was lying down on the floor, I remember looking up and seeing all the crowd's faces, and I remember looking 'round and seeing a big gorilla, just sitting there. After, I just fell back into unconsciousness."

"The fact that the child was unconscious basically brought out the tenderness, the caring, that's in a gorilla," says Andy. "I think he was very concerned for the child."

"It changed a lot of people's views on gorillas after it happened," remarks Brian Lelion. "After I videotaped this, I went home and just had a look to see what I had videotaped. Then it really sort of sunk into me what had really happened."

And what had happened was nothing short of a miracle. To have survived the thirty-foot fall was incredible, but the protective and caring nature of the giant gorilla was simply miraculous.

"I hope that people can understand a little more about

the way gorillas work. They'll use their strength and power when necessary, but not with children. They're nice. They're nice people. This is what I look on them as," declares Andy Wood. "I mean, they're just hairier than we are."

KITTY CPR

Firemen in Superior, Wisconsin, were shocked to hear the unexpected sound of kittens one day, as they cleaned up after a major fire. But when they located the animals, Lenny, one of the firefighters, says, "One of these kittens was in bad shape, showed no signs of life at all."

Nevertheless, no one had been injured in the fire that day, and Lenny was determined to keep it that way. He immediately began working to save the kitten's life, but firefighter Jim Lehikoinen had his doubts.

"I thought, I don't think this is gonna work," recalls Jim.

But Lenny refused to give up. He began CPR on the

kitten, theorizing that, "Based on the knowledge that I had for our fellow man, I used lighter breaths of air, lighter compressions on the chest. And watched for an air exchange to see if I could get some air to come out of the kitten's lungs."

Other firemen pitched in to help when they saw what Lenny was doing. "Well, I thought, if he's doing this, I'll go to the rig. I'll get our oxygen, and see if that'll help," says one. Spirits were raised when the kitten appeared to revive, briefly. "The first little shot, it kinda made a little jerk like it's gonna do some good, you know," remarks one of the firefighters. But, unfortunately, the reaction appeared to be involuntary, and the kitten continued not to breathe on its own.

"I kept with it, trying to do everything I could to save that kitten," says Lenny. "I started stimulating the kitten's spine by rubbing my fingernails on it to try and introduce some kind of pain or stimulus to make the kitten respond."

"Lenny would give it another little breath and then continue to do this procedure for what seemed like forever. Finally, I had to go back to my rig," remembers a fellow firefighter.

At this point, Jim came over. He'd seen how hard Lenny had been working, and he'd changed his mind about the kitten's chance of survival. "I figured, Well, Lenny's been there a long time, so we traded jobs, just to share the responsibilities of what was going on." The two men worked together to revive the tiny kitten. "I was a little concerned that we might blow too hard into the poor little animal and hurt him. But Lenny was real gentle and real careful," recalls Jim.

Lenny's job was to save lives, and this one had a special meaning for him; as he puts it, "I've had pets all my life. I know how important it is to have a pet, and to lose a pet.

"After about twelve or fourteen minutes, the kitten started moving its legs, taking breaths of air, and opening its eyes. I started to think to myself, Hey, this is great. There's a possibility that we're going to save this kitten," says Lenny.

Another fireman remarked, "I'd seen the kitten moving, the legs starting to kick, and I thought, Well, you know, this is a miracle."

And the miracle has a doubly happy ending. For not only did Lenny save a life, he found a new friend *for* life: he adopted the kitten, and named it Smudge—firemen's slang for "small fire."

Woman's Best Friend

Nestled among the majestic redwoods of Northern California is the quaint town of Garberville. In 1999, Nancy and Jeff Best were raising a family there, while running a popular coffee shop, the Java Joint.

"Our lives were a little hectic at the time," recalls Nancy. "We had three kids going to three different schools. My husband had taken a job in the Bay Area, which is a good four-and-a-half-hour drive away, so during the week he'd be gone and I would have to run the shop."

Even with her active schedule, however, Nancy dreamed of adding another member to her family.

"I've always been an animal lover," she says. "My mom

used to call me 'Dr. Doolittle' when I was little, because I always had animals around me.

"I'm particularly fond of dogs," says Nancy. "I had been pestering my husband about getting a yellow Lab every time I would see one. I would hint, 'Christmas is coming, I want a yellow Lab.' But he kept saying that we really shouldn't get one at that time."

"I didn't want a dog, because our lives were kind of in flux then," Jeff says. "We were renting the house and we just didn't need a dog."

But a few weeks before Christmas, opportunity rang.

"I received a phone call from a friend of mine who had spotted some yellow Labs," says Nancy. "She said, 'Nancy, these dogs are just beautiful. You have to come down here right now. The man who's selling them is just here for a minute, he's traveling. If you don't come now, you're going to miss your opportunity.'"

Nancy decided that she wasn't going to let the opportunity pass her by, and she took off to meet her friend without telling Jeff where she was headed.

"I got in the car and drove to the park," says Nancy, "and as I drove up, I saw these beautiful puppies. They were so cute, they were the most darling yellow Labs. They were healthy, and their tails were wagging, and they were all running around in a little bunch. I knew that I wasn't going to leave without a puppy.

"And at this point I didn't know if I wanted a boy or a girl," says Nancy, but she bonded instantly with one of the puppies. "When I held her, I knew she was the one I was going to take home."

"So anyway, she showed up with this puppy, and I was not happy about it at all," recalls Jeff. "I wanted her to take it back."

"Which I couldn't do, because the owner of the dogs had already left," counters Nancy. "So that worked out really well."

It didn't take long for the puppy to soften Jeff's hard heart.

"I mean, puppies, you know, you fall in love with a puppy almost immediately, so it worked out pretty good that way," admits Jeff.

Nancy named the pup Mia. And Mia grew to become a true member of the family.

"Mia's kind of like Nancy," says Jeff. "She likes to have fun, she likes to be with people. She's just a nice dog, always friendly, ready to cuddle up or be scratched behind the ear or whatever."

When Mia was about fourteen months old, Nancy started to feel run-down, and her dog's behavior began to change.

"With my life so hectic at that time, I was feeling a little tired. I was just getting worn out. I was physically tired. I knew if I didn't start taking a rest during the day I couldn't continue," says Nancy. "When I would lay on the couch, Mia would usually lay next to me, and it would be pretty uneventful. But during this particular time when I was starting to feel really tired, Mia would come up and lay her nose on my chest and start sniffing. And at the time I didn't think anything of it. I thought maybe she was smelling meat or some kind of food from the Java

Joint that I might have had still on my shirt," explains Nancy.

"This proceeded again. She came back to me a couple of days later, and did the same sniffing and licking in the same spot. I was so tired and I was so bothered by the fact that she was doing this, that I actually got mad and put her outside," Nancy admits.

And she kept her outside the next day as well, but eventually Mia snuck back into the house.

"My daughter had come home from school," says Nancy, "and after she opened the door, Mia came barreling into the house. She dove into my chest, with her nose again in the area she had been sniffing and licking before. I started to rub it with my hand, because it did cause a great deal of pain.

"And at that instant, I felt the lump."

"Despite having had a mammogram before that was negative, indeed there was a lump of tissue there that was new and different from the previous exams," reveals Nancy's physician, Dr. Mark Phelps. "Unfortunately, the lump did have the little specks of calcium that make us real suspicious."

Dr. Phelps recommended further testing to determine whether the lump was malignant.

"It was very scary," recalls Nancy. "I never thought I would get cancer. I always thought everybody else got cancer, and I lived a pretty healthy lifestyle. It was a shock."

"The diagnosis was, unfortunately, a new breast cancer

called ductal cancer," says Dr. Phelps. "It's one that can be extremely dangerous, that spreads quickly, and the timing is critical. Gotten early, these are the cancers you can cure, but just a little too late and they spread."

"When the doctor called me with the results," says Nancy, "the first thing that I thought was, I was going to lose my family, my children. I wouldn't get to see them grow. Other than the fact that you think you're going to die, you have to think about the things you haven't done yet. And you know tomorrow is not promised to anyone. I had that feeling in an instant."

Nancy was immediately scheduled for a partial mastectomy and the removal of nearby lymph nodes where the cancer might have spread.

"My fear was for any suffering Nancy might have to endure," says Jeff. "I gave her a kiss for good luck, and I was just trying to keep her positive. But, you know, there's always that thought in the back of your mind that you can't help but think: Your wife is going to die."

As Jeff waited, the surgeons removed twenty-six lymph nodes from below Nancy's arm.

"All of the lymph nodes were negative for any spread. The cancer was confined just to the small area," says Dr. Phelps. "She was able to remove the cancer and preserve her breasts, and go through the treatment with a very high likelihood of complete cure."

"If this cancer hadn't been detected at that time, my doctor feels that it could have gotten a lot worse. He said the chance of it spreading would've increased," reveals

Nancy. "Had Mia not discovered it at that time, my chances for survival would have been greatly reduced."

"The fact that the dog was able to do this is just remarkable," says Dr. Phelps. "I've heard little bits and hints. You hear them from cancer specialists now and again 'cause they'll hear the stories. But I never thought I would see a case like that. Who would ever think?"

"I think the miracle here," says Jeff, "was that Mia was determined to let Nancy know that there was something going on there that wasn't right, and she kept at it until Nancy realized it."

To show Mia how much they appreciate the miracle she gave them, Nancy and Jeff reward her each morning with a special treat.

"My husband makes breakfast for the kids in the morning, and Mia waits anxiously every day for her pancake," says Nancy. "And she's just thrilled to be spoiled like that. She's the little princess of the house now."

And Jeff realizes how close he came to not allowing her to be part of their family.

"I thought about the fact that I never wanted the dog to begin with, and what an amazing thing it was that we got her," Jeff remarks. "I mean, I didn't want it, and Nancy kind of snuck down there and bought this dog behind my back, and then it turns out to be a savior dog, you know. So it was a tremendous thing."

"For Mia to find this cancer, and just five months after I had a negative breast exam, is a miracle. It's nothing less than a miracle to me," declares Nancy. "If Mia could understand words, I would tell her thank you. Thank you for alerting me to something that could have taken my life, something that could have taken me away from my children, my husband, the things I love most.

"I would tell her that she is my miracle, and there is a reason that I have her, and that I love her."

ELEPHANTS NEVER FORGET

Shirley the Elephant was a veteran circus performer, traveling from town to town and entertaining the crowds night after night. But life in the center ring was far from glamorous. Animal advocate Carol Buckley explains:

"When you look at the simple needs of an elephant, they need room to roam, access to live vegetation, real food. If you look at elephants that travel, are they experiencing that? Let's take a day in the life of a traveling elephant and start in the morning. The elephant has to load into a trailer or a transport container. The animal is traveling either hours or days at a time. They're chained in one place. To me, the fact that elephants are chained at any time is neglectful. And it really borders on abusive."

The abuse begins the moment they're captured in the wild. It is especially hard on the most profitable and vulnerable catch of all—baby elephants.

Carol says, "There's a great injustice done to baby elephants that are separated from their mother, from their family. They would be continually pampered and touched and talked to, reassured and taught. And that's what baby elephants didn't get when they came into captivity."

In the mid-1970s, Shirley was joined under the big top by a recently captured baby elephant named Jenny. The terrified creature was drawn to Shirley's kind soul. But they became more than just friends. They forged a loving mother-daughter relationship.

Carol remembers, "Their relationship was very strong. It's amazing how loving and caring they were for each other."

And the bond continued to grow, until suddenly and without warning, Shirley's baby was taken away. It was another crushing blow in a life filled with torture and despair.

Jenny was sold to a breeding facility where she was severely crippled by a bull elephant, making her useless to her new owners. So she was sold again to a small traveling circus, where her health deteriorated.

Meanwhile, Shirley's life in the circus had also come to a bad end when she was attacked by another female elephant.

"She attacked Shirley from behind," says Carol, "and kept slamming her from behind. And Shirley couldn't get away because she was chained. And she actually broke her leg right where the chain was. Shirley went to the winter quarters to recover. And she didn't recover well enough that she could perform again. So the circus donated Shirley to the zoo."

It was the first good thing that had happened in Shirley's life. And the best part was that it led her into the loving care of Louisiana Purchase zookeeper Solomon James.

Solomon remembers, "My first encounter with Shirley the Elephant was something else. I felt like you do when you meet a girl and you don't know her, but you try to get yourself acquainted with this girl by doing some friendly things. I would see her, pass by her, I would work with her, I would say, 'Shirley, you doing all right?' And Shirley would respond, she'd turn around and hold out her trunk and I would pat her on the trunk and it was just great. She was my friend. Sometimes she would rub you on your face with her trunk to make sure you were the right one. An elephant never forgets you once it gets to know you."

For the next twenty-three years, Solomon and Shirley were inseparable.

Assistant zoo director Gary Hicks was especially impressed by their relationship.

"Solomon was very close to Shirley," Gary remembers. "She and Solomon had kind of a special bond between them."

But zoo officials knew that fifty-two-year-old Shirley missed the company of other elephants.

Gary says, "Shirley was a lone elephant, and most elephants are very sociable animals. So we tried to make a decision: Could we place her somewhere else? We came across the Elephant Sanctuary and a lady by the name of Carol Buckley."

Carol says, "I got a phone call one morning, and it was a curator from the zoo."

Gary said to her, "We have an elephant named Shirley. We're trying to find a great home for her and we read about you on the Internet." Later, he said, "I felt, after the first five minutes, that she had a genuine concern for elephants. So I felt from her standpoint that Shirley would be in the best possible place."

Carol says, "We were very receptive to Shirley coming. I came out and spent the day there. And, of course, I was enchanted by Shirley because she's just amazing."

The hardest part would be breaking the news to Solomon that Shirley was leaving.

"I guess I wanted her to stay," Solomon says. "It would be nice if she would just stay, you know, and we continue our bond. But then I looked at the second part and said, Well, it would be nice if she did move to something better. This was my friend, and I wanted her to have something better."

And so, arrangements were made to move Shirley to the Elephant Sanctuary. It would be a day of laughter and tears and an astonishing discovery that would change Shirley's life forever.

Solomon says, "I came into work knowing that this was going to happen. I saw Shirley look like she was ready, you know. And I asked myself the question, Am I ready?"

For the first time in twenty-three years, Solomon would have to put his dear friend in chains.

Solomon calmed the frightened elephant, saying, "Come on, Shirley, nothing's going to happen. We're gonna take you to a new place where you can meet other elephants, and I'll be with you." And Shirley moved calmly into the trailer.

"I wanted to follow Shirley all the way to Tennessee," says Solomon, " 'cause I wanted to be sure that everything was all right. I wanted to be sure that she knew that I was still there, and that I was with her all the way. I stood in the enclosure where she was going to come in off the truck."

Carol talked to her gently, and Solomon said, "Finally, Shirley began to back up. You wouldn't believe it. It was like a big fanfare. Reporters were there with cameras, and they had a great big basket full of food. I mean, the best looking hay that you ever want to see. Baskets full of goodies. It was like a birthday party for Shirley."

In a wonderfully symbolic moment, Solomon took off the last chains Shirley would ever wear. It was a moment he would never forget.

"I felt moved. I felt so moved about it, until I said to myself, Now I've set my friend free. She can go out and roam, do what she wants to do. I looked out across the sanctuary, and I said, 'Shirley, this is yours now. This is all yours. The chain is gone.' I told her, 'Let me just keep this chain to remind me that I was the last one to unchain you. And I was the one who set you free.' "

Shirley's first day at the sanctuary was going well, but

her adventures were far from over. That night, another elephant entered the barn and began acting strangely.

Carol says, "She came into the barn from the far end, so she was three stalls away. She started pacing the stall and reaching out, and being very anxious and agitated. And her focus was completely on Shirley."

Carol decided to move the two elephants closer together, but continued to separate them by a railing.

"She would get down and reach like she wanted Shirley in the stall with her," Carol remembers. "She kept going back and forth, and back and forth. And Shirley was very calm. And she was standing with her body parallel along the corral. And she was allowing herself to be touched, but she was only marginally interested."

And then, suddenly, something magical happened.

"It was like a light went on in Shirley's eye," Carol says. "She stopped and she kinda turned her head a little funny and her eyes got really big. And then she went trumpet, trumpet, trumpet. And with that, she started to bellow. She just started screaming this long sort of primal yell. It just vibrated the barn. It was so intense that it was on the verge of frightening."

For the next few moments, Carol held her breath. Was she about to witness an attack? Or was something else going on? The answer was nothing short of miraculous.

"In a perfect world, we always want elephants to meet in a big space. That wasn't going to happen here. These two girls were gonna have to meet inside because they wouldn't go away from each other. We opened the gate.

Here they were, these two crippled ladies, they just glided toward each other and just sort of melted into each other. And then they were side by side, always touching some part of the other's body. What we felt was, obviously this wasn't a new relationship developing, this was an old relationship. These elephants knew each other. Now I wanted to know *how* they knew each other."

Over the next few days, Carol went to work unearthing both elephants' histories. To her amazement, she discovered that they had performed in the same circus together, twenty-three years earlier. Even more astonishing was the identity of the other elephant: It was Shirley's long-lost friend, Baby Jenny.

Carol says, "Yeah, it's been twenty-three years, but I know darn well that Jenny knew Shirley when she walked into the barn. She recognized Shirley, maybe Shirley looked the same to her. But I think it goes deeper than that. I think Jenny knew it was Shirley because Shirley had such a powerful impact on her when she was a baby."

Together, Mother Shirley and her surrogate daughter Jenny spend every moment, day and night, at each other's side.

Carol says, "Jenny and Shirley's relationship today is almost identical to when they finally were allowed in together. They are constant companions. Jenny is obviously the baby. Shirley is a very nurturing, mothering influence on Jenny. But Shirley and Jenny have a special connection, and it's a joy to know that they get to have this for the rest of their lives, that they are never, ever gonna be separated again."

Solomon says, "Shirley met a friend that she once knew. Someone that was once close to her, and now here they are reunited. She's living like an elephant should live. I miss her. She probably misses me. But I have the joy of knowing she's happy. That makes me feel good."

REMARKABLE RESCUES

ＳECOND CHANCE ANGEL

1999 was a bad year for Rob Gingery of Memphis, Tennessee. Recently divorced, and separated from his son, Rob channeled his depression into motorcycles and living on the edge.

"He was at the point in his life where he didn't care anymore. He'd party all the time, and then he'd want to know where the next party was," remembers his girlfriend Cale Smith. "He was always cutting up on his motorcycle—the faster, the better."

And then one afternoon in May, Rob and Cale were leaving a restaurant along with Rob's close friend, Randy Brewer.

"Rob and I were going to ride our bikes over to his house. Cale was riding with another friend of ours in their car," explains Randy.

After the couple said their good-byes, Randy and Rob sped out of the parking lot. As they headed back to Rob's house, the two friends played a dangerous cat-and-mouse game, each trying to outrace the other at speeds of up to a hundred miles per hour.

Randy recalls, "We were hot-rodding back and forth, you know, on the main streets. When we got in the neighborhood, we turned the corner and Rob just shot off. I wasn't really familiar with all the streets, so I drove at kind of a slower pace."

Meanwhile, Cale and her friend Kat had taken a different route to Rob's house.

"We went kind of the back road, and as we got there I noticed that his motorcycle wasn't there. I looked at Kat and I said, 'He's down.' She told me not to jump to conclusions, but I knew he was down, I could feel it."

The two women sped off in search of Rob and Randy to make sure they were all right, but they didn't have to travel far to discover that Cale's horrible premonition had come true.

"When we turned the corner, there he was. The motorcycle was flipped upside down, and pipes were sticking out. It was a mess. Rob was lying on the curb with blood all over him."

"Cale was hysterical," remembers Randy. "She was crying, hanging over him, trying to see if he was alive."

"The paramedics came at about the same time, and they jumped out and pulled me away from him," says Cale. "We didn't know if he had a broken neck—we didn't know anything. When the paramedics finally got him on the gurney, Rob kept saying, 'Where's Cale? Where's Cale?' He looked at me and gestured for me to give him a kiss, so I leaned down and gave him one, and then he shut his eyes. I thought he'd died. I really thought that was it."

Rob was still alive, but badly injured. The paramedics rushed him to the Regional Medical Center in Memphis. His injuries were extensive, including four skull fractures, a broken hand, and a broken leg. But it was his behavior that had Dr. Preston Miller most concerned.

"It's pretty typical for folks who have a significant head injury to be combative or confused or a little bit out of it," Dr. Miller explains, "so he went from our shock trauma room to the CAT-scan room, where he had a CAT scan of his brain."

The CAT scan revealed that Rob had received a traumatic head injury. A small blood clot had formed in his brain.

"Those sometimes stay the same and sometimes get worse," says Dr. Miller. "There's no way of knowing. If they stay the same, it's great, but if they enlarge, it either leads to serious brain damage or death."

Cale was there when they did another CAT scan early the next day. "By about 7:00 in the morning, the blood clot had tripled in size. So the doctors rushed in and started telling us that they needed to do emergency surgery."

Rob was rushed to an operating room where neuro-surgeons spent the next several hours opening his skull and removing the blood clot from his brain. When they finished, there was nothing left to do but wait and pray that Rob would regain consciousness.

Meanwhile, Cale struggled to deal with the grim possibilities. "The doctors came out and said he could be a vegetable. I thought about what I would do if he did die. I cried more than anybody knew. Not only was I going to lose the person I was with, but Rob's also my best friend. I never gave up hope on him, though. We prayed, and we prayed, and we prayed."

Miraculously, two and a half hours after the surgery, Cale's prayers were answered.

Rob remembers, "I wake up, and I'm in a room by myself. I've got hoses and IVs hanging off me, and I don't have a clue as to where I'm at. I don't remember having a wreck. Then the nurse walks in and tells me to be still, and all I can say is 'What am I doing here?'"

"He got better like overnight," Cale marvels. "I mean, he had brain surgery on Monday and was at home in bed by Friday. It was totally miraculous that he recovered the way he did."

But as astounding as his physical recovery was, it was nothing compared to the life-altering change that had taken place in Rob's attitude.

"I had a whole new perception, a whole new feeling inside. I felt clean. This wreck was the best bad thing that ever happened to me because it was a reality check. It sobered me up, straightened me up."

But there was still one nagging question in his mind.

"When you hear about a child that dies in a car wreck or about anyone that passes away, you wonder why a person like me was saved. You wonder, Why am I here? Was it just an accident that I lived?"

Rob underwent a remarkable transformation. With a newfound sense of purpose, Rob channeled his energy from motorcycles and parties to starting his own business as an electrical contractor.

Rob said, "I believe that prior to the wreck I would not have been able to handle the business. I would like to say I'm on my way back up and I thank God every day."

But Rob still wondered why he of all people would be given a second chance at life, and then, almost a year to the day after his accident, Rob was driving past the same intersection when he received the answer to his question.

"I was heading back to the office in a dead run—you know, in a hurry. I come up, and there's a car wreck right in front of me," recalls Rob. "I mean, two trucks hit each other right in front of me. I was the first one on the scene."

Rob ran to the nearest vehicle while calling 911 on his cell phone. Meanwhile, inside the other vehicle, Vicky O'Briant was just beginning to regain consciousness.

Vicky remembers, "I didn't know anything about how we had flipped over or anything. I just knew that I was upside down, and I really couldn't get a grasp on where I actually was."

When Rob was certain the first driver was okay, he turned his attention to Vicky's truck.

"With truck damage as bad as that, you don't know

what you're fixing to find. You're praying that a cop might show up, because I don't want to do it. I managed to get the driver of the vehicle to the curb. I sat her down on the grass, and the little boy sat down right beside her."

"That's when I started screaming about my daughter, Camille," says Vicky, "that my daughter was hurt very badly."

Rob rushed back to the vehicle. "I look in, and there is a little girl, upside down, unconscious, and just hanging limp with the seat belt around her neck. Her lips and skin were exactly the same color—she was one solid color blue."

Worse still, the truck was leaking fluid and the engine was still running. Rob knew that if he didn't act quickly, the truck would catch fire or explode.

"There was no room inside the truck. It was crushed and I couldn't get the seat belt unbuckled. At this point, I'm now praying, 'Please don't let this truck blow up.' I'm throwing a double prayer up to God—'Please don't let this baby die, whatever you do, please don't let this baby die. And please don't let the truck blow up.' Luckily, I had a small Leatherman pocketknife on me and I was able to use that to cut the seat belt."

Rob quickly cut the young girl free. But she remained unconscious.

"I had this little child lying in front of me. And I really didn't want to move her because I thought she might have some internal injuries. So I decided I would stay inside the truck with her and pray that an ambulance or somebody would show up."

Vicky was beside herself. "I didn't know anything about what was going on—if my daughter was okay. And I was so scared that I was just screaming. I didn't know how to help her. I just knew that somebody was in there helping my daughter."

After ten terrifying minutes, paramedics finally arrived. Luckily, the truck never caught on fire, and the paramedics were able to get Camille out. With the situation finally under control, Rob left the scene without a word. Vicky and her children were taken to a local hospital. Miraculously, no one had suffered any serious injuries, including her daughter, Camille.

"The doctors told me that if someone hadn't cut her out of that seat belt, she would have suffocated," says Vicky. "There was no way that she probably would have made it."

But Vicky had no way of thanking the heroic stranger that had saved their lives that day...until she stumbled upon a clue to his identity.

"A few days later we decided we were going to clean the truck and get our personal possessions out. We looked in the backseat and there was a Leatherman knife that we'd never seen before, and I said, 'This must be the knife that cut my daughter out of her seat belt.' So I turned it over and there was a man's name on it. When I got home, I looked in the phone book and the man's name was right there. It was the only Rob Gingery that there was."

Rob was working at home when the telephone rang. Little did he know, it was Vicky O'Briant.

"And she said, 'Were you at the scene of an accident?' and I said, 'Yes.' Then she said, 'I've got something that belongs to you. We found your knife in the truck.'"

Vicky recalls, "I gave him my name, and I said, 'Well, I believe you're the man who saved my daughter.' And he couldn't believe that she had made it, and that he had been a part of saving her life. It was a miracle to him, and he couldn't wait to meet us."

But it was Vicky who was truly in disbelief when she learned about Rob's motorcycle wreck at that same intersection just one year before.

"I couldn't believe that he happened upon our accident at the same site where he had his. I felt like his survival was such a miracle and that God let him live for a reason, and that reason was to help my daughter and save my daughter's life. He says he's not a hero, but I believe he's my hero, and he's my daughter's hero."

Little Camille agrees. "I think it's a miracle because he saved us and if he wouldn't have been there, I would have died."

Today, Rob is a close friend to Vicky and her family, and while it took a year and two near-tragedies to bring them together, the experience they share taught them all the lesson of a lifetime.

"I don't go to church every Sunday," says Vicky. "But I do pray to God every day, and thank Him for saving us and saving Rob a year ago."

"Prior to my wreck, I took the blessings I've had in life for granted," concludes Rob. "I don't do that anymore.

The lessons I've had in the last eighteen months have taught me to look at things differently. Even when they seem their worst, look around, because it could be worse. Every day, I take time to say, 'Thank you, God, thank you for what I've got.' "

*L*ADY IN THE LAKE

Ever since he was a young boy, Paul Lessard's nightmare was always the same.

"I'm in a car, and the car hurtles through the air, and then hits the water. And the water starts coming into the car and we start submerging. And I can feel the water moving up my legs, up to my waist, up to my chest. These dreams began when I was eleven years old, and literally continued three–four times a year, all the way up until I was in my thirties," says Paul.

His wife, Jayne, a psychologist, was concerned as well, often waking in the night when he had a nightmare to ask, "Honey, are you okay? Did you have another one of those drowning dreams? Baby, I don't know what's causing them." Frustrated, Jayne attempted to help Paul understand his dream, but although they'd "talk through it and stuff, it didn't ever feel like there was a real resolution to why he was having it or what was going on—and it would keep recurring."

Then in April of 1993, Paul left his home early one morning during a downpour.

"The rain was so heavy, it was like the windshield wipers weren't even working that day. I didn't realize it, but it had been raining like that all night long. I was on my way to play squash and I was running late. So when I hit Main Street, I remembered a shortcut that I had discovered a couple of weeks before," Paul explains.

But what Paul didn't know was the "shortcut" would take him down a road where, just minutes earlier, a flash flood had carried a car into the lake. Luckily, Jack Kavanagh was nearby.

"I ran down to the edge of the water and dove in and started swimming out to the car," says Jack. "The water was powerful. I get to the car and there's a lady inside."

More determined than ever to help, Jack swam around the car, trying to find a way to help the woman out. "And I'm swimming around and I'm trying to get the doors open and nothing is happening. I realized that the car was filling with water and the person inside was in great danger. At that point I was really praying; what should I do?"

It was then that Paul Lessard arrived on the scene.

"I could see a man on top of a car," Paul says. "I

thought he was the driver and maybe couldn't swim. I literally started taking off my clothes at that second to go help him."

Paul rushed into the water to assist, but when he reached Jack, Jack explained the situation to him. "At that point he told me that he was fine but there was a woman trapped in the car, and he needed my help. He couldn't break the window."

Both men struggled to open the car doors, but some were locked shut, and even those that weren't couldn't be forced open against the water pressure. It soon became obvious to Paul that if they were going to save this woman, he needed to run to find something they could use to break open a window. Paul says, "My thought was to strip down to get in the water, then run to a house to get something to break the window."

While Jack stayed behind to do everything he could to help the woman trapped in the car, Paul took off in search of the nearest house. Amazingly, when he got there, the woman who answered the door did not turn away the drenched man standing in his shorts outside her door at 5:00 A.M.

"She let me into her house," recalls Paul with wonder. "I ran to this tool room, where I grabbed a plumber's wrench and a hammer, and I turned around and ran out as quick as I could. And I called back to her to call 911."

Back at the car, the situation was getting worse by the minute.

"I could see the water gushing in through the vents

and filling the car up," says Jack. "So the first thought was, I have to get her out of her seat belt, because if this car sinks and she's in her seat belt, it would be nearly impossible to get her out of it." Luckily, the woman trapped inside was finally able to pop the seat belt loose—and not a moment too soon.

"The water was very deep and the front end of the car was going down," Jack says. "There was an air pocket in the back of the car, and I said to her, 'I can't get the door open, you have to go in the back. Just calm down. I'm going to go to the back.' She started to climb over the front seat and head to the back of the car. I could see the car filling up with water and realized how urgent a situation this was turning into, because she only had a few seconds of air left."

With time running out and the car sinking fast—and just as the woman's oxygen supply was nearly exhausted—Paul Lessard returned to the water's edge.

"All I can remember hearing was the roar of the water, the rain, and my heart beating. My heart was just pounding out of my chest and I was convinced I was going to have a heart attack doing this. When I got up on the bumper and looked into the window, she was submerged in water. She wasn't breathing. And I remember thinking, God don't let us get this close and not let us save her. After I see that this woman is drowning, I looked over to this man and yelled at him to cover his eyes." With that, Paul bravely broke the car window.

"And we started trying to get her out as fast as we

could because the car was really going down quickly," says Paul.

"It sank all of a sudden," Jack agrees. "In one big moment, we were all three completely under water." The two men held on tight to the woman, and swam laboriously to shore.

"The water was so murky that we knew if we let her go, we'd never find her again," explains Paul. "We fought to get through the current and when we got her up to shore, one of us must have elbowed her, because she started regurgitating all this water...."

Thanks to the neighbor who'd loaned Paul the tools and called 911, the paramedics showed up just moments later. The woman had swallowed a large amount of water, but the paramedics were optimistic about her recovery. They said to her, "We'll get you to the hospital and get some help with that breathing. How about that? Get some of that water out."

"I don't think you can describe what it's like to save someone's life," says Paul. "I mean, it's amazing."

"I was just very, very relieved that she was safe," adds Jack.

It's been seven years since Paul and Jack rescued Ella Mae Bowman, and they continue to be in awe of the miracle that brought them together.

"The confluence of the timing and the people—two men that could swim, who happened to be there at 5:00 A.M. on a rainy April morning.... That to me is miraculous," marvels Jack.

"If it hadn't been for them—Paul and Jack—I wouldn't be here today. They were my angels and got me out of that car," Ella Mae says.

As Paul puts it, "If you don't believe in miracles before an event like this happens in your life, you absolutely do afterward." For Paul, the incident brought another miracle as well, and it gave him a profound respect for the mysterious ways we can affect each other's lives.

"From the day we rescued Ella Mae, I have never had another nightmare about a car in the water. The only thing I can say is that this whole event healed me, I guess, of all the fears I had." He muses, "At that moment in time, we held someone's life in our hands. And it was a precious woman's life; a woman who had children and grandchildren. In the years that have passed, I look back and I go, Gosh, what would have happened if we hadn't saved her?

"And I thank God that we did."

JENNIFER'S INSTINCT

On September 30, 1998, John Muller was returning to his home in DeQueen, Arkansas, after spending several days in Minnesota on business. John suffered from severe back pain, often so excruciating that it would paralyze him, but the spinal specialists he'd consulted could offer no cure.

It was almost midnight, and two hours into his drive along a rural highway, when John's back began to spasm.

"My left leg started to cramp, and then I got a massive spasm," recalls John. "It just literally took my breath away...that's the last I remember." He lost control of his pickup truck, which then went over an embankment and crashed under the Holly Creek Bridge. The next thing

John knew, he was trapped in the dark beneath the wreckage, immobilized by pain and drifting in and out of consciousness.

"My first memory was looking out of the vehicle, and wondering why I was in a cave," says John. Paralyzed with pain, he prayed. "I said, 'Lord, I need help. I cannot move.'"

Although the pain was unbearable, there was nothing John could do but wait and pray that someone would find him.

The next morning, a school bus was traveling the same route that John had taken the night before. On board, twelve-year-old Jennifer Turner was thinking about the upcoming school day. As she gazed out the window, something caught her eye.

"It was a white truck, and it was facing upward. You could see a little bit of the windshield, and it was broken," recalls Jennifer.

Jennifer immediately sensed that something was wrong, but when she approached the bus driver and told him what she had seen, he refused to stop. His theory was that someone was probably just fishing down there.

"It didn't feel right, the truck sittin' way down there. . . . I couldn't even see anybody down there fishing, and there was no road down there," says Jennifer. "And I thought nobody would really play down there because they'd get stuck."

Once her school day began, Jennifer focused on her studies. She didn't think about the truck under the bridge again until that afternoon on the bus ride home. Coming from the opposite direction, however, the angle was not as good, and though she strained to see, Jennifer didn't have a good view of the spot.

"I was trying to look out the window, but it was too close to the side of the bridge that you couldn't see it," she explains. "I just thought I'd see it in the mornin' if it was down there."

Trapped beneath the Holly Creek Bridge for over twelve hours now, John was having sharper back spasms than ever, compounded by injuries from the accident. John was in so much pain that most of the time, he wasn't even aware of the vehicles passing overhead.

"I was in and out of consciousness," says John. "I could remember trying to move one time but the pain was just too much, it was almost like I couldn't catch my breath, and I would pass out."

That afternoon, Jennifer tried to tell her mother, Becky Turner, what she'd seen.

"When she came home from school, she seemed kinda worried," Becky recalls. "She said, 'Momma, there's a truck down by the bridge.' She said, 'Don't you think we should look into it?'

"I brushed it off," Becky admits. "I told her that somebody probably was fishing down by the bridge." Becky told her daughter that if she noticed the truck again the next day, then maybe they would talk about it.

"She wouldn't listen to me, nobody would," states Jennifer. "It made me mad, so I just went to my room."

Twenty-five miles down the highway, in DeQueen,

John's wife, Paula Muller, grew increasingly worried about her husband. He was twenty-four hours overdue.

"My biggest fear, as time went on, was they wouldn't find him alive," she reveals.

Two of the Mullers' sons had been out searching for John all day, without finding a trace of him. The airline confirmed that he had arrived on his flight from Minnesota, and a search of airport parking lots revealed that John's pickup truck had left the airport.

"The boys got to where they didn't really want to drive up in the driveway to look at the expression on my face," says Paula. "They'd look up at the door, and they'd put their heads down, and I knew then that they hadn't seen or heard anything."

That night, Paula prayed for the safety of her husband as she had never prayed before. "My time spent here was praying," she says, "asking God to please let the boys find him alive, that he would be okay."

That same night, Jennifer also said a prayer.

"I prayed for whoever was in the truck, that they would be okay until I could tell somebody who would listen to me and check it out."

But would her prayer be answered? And would anyone believe the intuition of a twelve-year-old child?

On the morning of Friday, October 2, Jennifer Turner crossed the bridge for the third time—hoping that the truck would be gone. But nothing had changed.

"Everything was the same. It was in the exact same spot, so I knew there was something wrong," recalls

Jennifer. She pleaded again with the bus driver to pull over, but he told her that there was no safe place for the bus to stop.

That day at school, she tried to alert a teacher after class, but she says, "I don't think he believed me. You know, he just thought it was my imagination." Frustrated, she says, "It made me mad that nobody was listening."

Now having endured more than thirty-six hours without food and water, John was increasingly feeling the effects of hunger and dehydration.

"I prayed," he says. "After that I didn't worry anymore. I just figured it was in God's hands. Either you're going to be with Him, or you're going to rejoin your family."

On Saturday, fifty-six hours since John's accident, Jennifer was about to cross the bridge for the fifth time in three days, this time in her grandfather's car with her younger brother and her mother.

"As we got closer to the bridge, she kept asking her grandpa to stop," says Becky. "She was very persuasive." Jennifer badgered her grandfather, crying and insisting that the truck was still stuck underneath the bridge. Finally, Becky says, "We got about a half mile down the road and he goes, 'All right, I'm gonna turn around and show you there isn't a truck underneath the bridge.'"

But the moment they pulled over next to the bridge and got out, they could see John's truck clearly. Becky went down the embankment to the wreckage, to see if anyone was inside the pickup.

"I could see the truck and that there's somebody in

there," she recalls. "As I went down, I kept on saying, 'Sir, can you hear me?' He just never responded. And I got closer to the truck and he kind of looked at his hand out the window, on the passenger side. And that's when I hollered at them on top of the bridge to go get help."

John Muller arrived at the hospital with a broken nose, cracked ribs, and a collapsed lung. He had gone nearly three days and nights without food or water, all the time enduring excruciating pain. He believes it's a miracle he's alive.

"If there wasn't a miracle from above, there is no way that I would be talking at this point," declares John.

"God had his angels out, and Jennifer was one of the angels to help find John," agrees Paula.

It turned out that John's sons had driven over the Holly Creek Bridge many times in their search. But only Jennifer, from her high seat in the bus, could see him.

Jennifer visited a heavily bandaged John in the hospital a few hours after his rescue. "He looked like he wanted to hug me and didn't want to let go. But he couldn't because he was still hurting," Jennifer remembers. "He kissed my hand. And called me his little guardian angel."

"When we pray to God, He's always listening to you," says Jennifer, "and if you believe, He answers them. And I believe. And He answered."

KIDNAP RESCUE ON I-5

On the afternoon of April 30, 1999, Detective Al Aldez arrived at an apartment building in Van Nuys, California—the scene of a suspected kidnapping. The victim was a five-year-old child named Joanna. Her mother, Delmi Estrada, was the only witness.

"During our conversation with Ms. Estrada, she told us how the crime occurred," remembers Detective Aldez. "The suspect was a male transient who basically lived at the apartment, and was allowed to stay there by doing odd jobs for the tenants at the apartment."

That morning he was helping Delmi move some possessions.

"This is something that the suspect had done before. Joanna asked her mother if she could accompany him down to the van; having done this before and nothing happening, she agreed to let Joanna go with him," explains Detective Aldez.

But this time the little girl didn't return. The man managed to lure Joanna into the van and drive away unseen.

Delmi recalls, "My window is facing the parking lot, so I went and looked through the blinds, and the van wasn't there."

"Being a typical parent, Delmi was distraught, emotionally upset for allowing herself to trust so much in this person whom she knew very little about," says Detective Aldez. "Was he married, single, divorced? Did he have children? Did he have a drug and alcohol history, or any criminal history? Being a parent myself, and members of the unit also have small children, our main concern was that nothing happened to the little girl."

Knowing that if the child wasn't found in the first twenty-four hours, she might never be, Detective Aldez alerted the California Highway Patrol, the FBI, and local press, radio, and television.

"On a case like this, it was very important that we have the public's assistance in locating the suspect."

But twenty-four hours came and went without a solid lead.

"I wanted to see her alive," Delmi recalls. "I asked for patience, and asked God to give me strength."

Forty-eight hours after the abduction, Mike and Colleena McHugh stopped for breakfast on their way home to San Francisco after attending an event sponsored by the National Rifle Association.

Mike remembers, "We were down for the weekend at the Great Western Show, which is a family cultural event celebrating the history of the country."

"Friends of ours who live in the L.A. basin heard about the kidnapping on the local news and television," explains Colleena. "And at the show, we were talking about it."

"There's an article about this kidnapping that the guys from the gun show were talking about," adds Mike. "An old friend of mine who'd been a policeman for twenty years mentioned that these kids seldom survive past three days when they're kidnapped like this. All I knew was that this was a bad guy who had a little girl. And to me that is one of the worst crimes you can commit."

The license plate number was mentioned in the article Mike was reading.

"And he decided to memorize it," recalls Colleena. "And we would make a concerted effort to look for the car."

Even knowing the license number, their odds of crossing paths with the kidnapper were over one in seven million—the number of vehicles on California's roads. But fifteen minutes back out on the highway, the odds were about to improve.

"There was a white Ford Aerostar traveling rather slowly in the right lane," explains Mike.

"And he said, 'That's it, that's it.' I couldn't believe my eyes," Colleena remembers with wonder.

Mike continues, "I could see the driver looking around nervously, and a small person in the right seat. So I made like I was having some car trouble with my truck and pulled over to the shoulder and let the kidnapper go by, then I pulled out behind him and followed him for a while, while being able to keep the van in sight ahead."

Meanwhile, Colleena called 911.

"At first he didn't believe that I had just read the license plate and the paper and that we had just passed the vehicle."

But she quickly persuaded him that she was telling the truth.

"He came back on the line and asked me if we would be willing to follow because there were no police within sixty miles."

Mike recalls, "At that point I knew that, well, it was up to us to keep this guy in sight, and we were going to be Joanna's lifeline."

As Mike and Colleena McHugh tailed the van, the police were marshaling forces from near and far. California Highway Patrol Officer Axel Reyes was just starting duty when he got the call.

"When I found out it was a little girl, it just hit home. My wife was pregnant at the time . . . and I was just thinking, you know, if my family member was in that situation . . ."

As Officer Reyes sped toward I-5, the 911 dispatcher

told Colleena they were sending patrol cars from the opposite direction to meet them. But it might take longer than they'd hoped. It was at that moment that the man they were following began driving erratically.

"The kidnapper's vehicle started drifting around a bit as if he were doing something in the van, which made us very nervous," says Colleena. "My worst fear was that he was harming the little girl because he realized someone was following him."

After nearly an hour on the road, the couple started feeling the strain.

Colleena remembers, "It was very stressful and it was very frightening to think it might not end like the movies end. It might not end happy."

After several agonizing minutes, Mike finally saw that help was on the way.

"I've never seen a more beautiful sight. The patrol car pulled alongside us and he gave me a wave. That was quite a relief at that point. The kidnapper still hadn't figured it out for sure and he was still driving along like he had been. After another ten minutes or so, two officers came from the other side of the freeway. They crossed the median behind us."

Officer Axel Reyes adds, "We turned on our lights and sirens. Once the suspect saw our lights he picked it up to about eighty, eighty-five miles an hour."

When it became clear that the suspect had no intention of stopping, Officer Reyes and the CHP moved into an offensive mode. They contacted a unit several miles ahead and instructed them to throw down a spike strip—a device designed to puncture the tires of the suspect's vehicle. Moments later, the speeding van hit the nail-studded steel strip.

"All we see is just dirt flying up and down, his van going up and down and just the dirt flying," recalls Officer Reyes.

Within seconds, the patrol cars had the suspect boxed in and officers were taking their positions. But the suspect wasn't going to give up that easily.

"I really got afraid, at this point, 'cause now the bad guy's got the little girl in the van...and he's not letting her go, he's not coming out," remembers Mike.

"The horrible part was sitting there thinking, We have come this far, yet it could all go terribly wrong right in front of us, 'cause this was not yet over," adds Colleena.

Finally, after what seemed like an interminable standoff, the subject emerged from the van.

"She just came to me," Officer Reyes recalls. "And I put her in the patrol vehicle, and had another officer just kind of watch over her."

And moments later, the kidnapper surrendered.

"He just kind of seemed confused and kind of dazed, and not really sure what was going on," says Officer Reyes.

The police took Raul Rodriguez into custody. Later, Detective Aldez learned the chilling truth about the kidnapper's motive.

"He told me that he kidnapped Joanna Lopez because he was in love with her, just like any man would be in love with a woman."

Fortunately, he had been stopped before he could harm her. And later that day, Joanna was joyfully reunited with her mother.

Delmi remembers, "I felt a lot of excitement. I was very happy just to have found her—very fortunate to have found my daughter again."

"It's a good feeling knowing that everything turned out the way it did," reflects Officer Reyes.

"Someone up there was watching over Joanna," adds Detective Aldez.

And they sent her two angels—Colleena and Mike McHugh.

Mike remarks, "It was a miracle that there they were on the freeway, and I had memorized the details so I was certain it was them. . . . and you might say, sometimes a miracle happens when preparedness meets opportunity."

A week later, the McHughs were presented with a Good Samaritan award for their successful rescue of Joanna. They also got to meet the little girl and her mother.

"We got to hug her and kiss her and we saw that she was fine, and the mother was very, very grateful," remembers Colleena. "It was just lovely to meet her, she was just a darling little girl."

"The McHughs were the salvation of my daughter," concludes Delmi. "And I really appreciate it and thank you. That's all I can say is thank you."

Avalanche Rescue

For Methodist minister David Moss, the best part of every winter is an annual weekend ski trip called "Snow Madness."

"It's been a highlight of my life every year, to do this with these guys," he says. Particularly with his good friend and fellow pastor, Dennis Eucalyptus. "We have known each other for over twenty years, and he has been going on Snow Madness trips for almost that length of time," David laughs.

The annual excursion usually follows the same routine from year to year. "We leave on Thursday and stay there for the weekend, and on Sunday, we always end with a special service with communion, and then ski back down to the cars," describes David.

But even though the group of friends all promised to meet again the following year for the 21st Annual Snow Madness trip, it didn't work out as planned.

"Normally, there's a big group of us going. But everybody canceled that year, and Dennis and I ended up the only two. The smallest annual in our history," says David.

The two men chose to climb Mount Lassen, a national park near David's Northern California home.

"We had checked the weather channel," David says. "They said it would be fine weather until Sunday, and that there would be some precipitation on Sunday. But since that was the morning of the day we were going to leave, we decided to go ahead."

David and Dennis made their way up the mountain, heading for a point three and a half miles above the trail head, where they planned to set up camp.

"We could not have picked a better day. It was just gorgeous up there," recalls David. "Being out there is such a special feeling. It's a spiritual feeling for me. It gives you a sense of serenity. No interruptions, nothing to draw your attention away from the beauty and simplicity." He adds, "It's very healing."

But by the next morning, the weather had made a sudden and dramatic change. They awoke to find a heavy snow falling outside their tents.

"The snow was coming in at a sort of slant, in big flakes. So that's the first time I had a little anxiety about this storm. It was coming in earlier and stronger than we expected. And there was still lots to do," remembers David. "I told Dennis we'd better get going, have our breakfast, pack everything together, do the communion, and get the heck out of there."

But as the two pastors performed their communion, the snow was covering the tracks they had made the day before.

"We left about ten o'clock in the morning, in the blizzard. The snow was flying in our faces. It created a kind of a disorientation, where you couldn't tell up from down," describes David.

With the severe weather, and without tracks to follow, the men were thrown off course. They found themselves heading straight into avalanche territory.

"We were gonna have to go through that avalanche area to get home," David realized, "and I was really beginning to worry that we were in some danger here."

As an added precaution, the men decided to tie on avalanche cords. "The theory is," explains David, "if there's an avalanche, these cords will kind of float to the top. And anyone who survives can see the cord and follow it to your buried body."

But David couldn't find his cord right away, and he told Dennis that he'd be right behind him. Dennis started out ahead.

"I got myself together and started behind him," says David. "I remember Dennis entering the avalanche field. And, in a very calm way, he said something like 'Time to advance.' I assumed that he meant 'I'd like you to lead now.' So I picked up my pace a little bit, watching his tracks. And then I got the shock of my life—because all of a sudden, I realized his tracks disappeared. That's when I realized that what he had said was *avalanche*." He pauses. "And he was gone.

"I had a whistle and I blew it," David asserts, "but he didn't return the call. I looked into the teeth of the storm as far as I could for evidence of his cord, or a hat, or a glove, or anything. There was nothing.

"I realized he was under me somewhere, somewhere. And he was dying."

Fortunately, David was able to use his cell phone to call for help—but it would take at least an hour before rescuers could arrive.

"I knew that if I didn't reach him within thirty minutes, most people die," says David. "I figured I only had one good chance to reach him before he died, and I didn't know where to start. I didn't have a clue. I prayed to God: Where do I start?"

David stuck his skis into the ground in the shape of an X, the international symbol for help, and began to dig madly in the snow. "I began where his tracks disappeared, and I looked frantically for that cord, for an item of clothing, for anything. Any clue.

"And the time went on ticking," says David. "I could imagine him struggling in there. He had to be somewhere below me, gasping for breath."

As David dug frantically for the next two hours, his exposure to the cold began to take its toll.

"I was beginning to lose strength. I was starting to shiver uncontrollably," he recalls. "I didn't think he'd be alive, but even if he wasn't, I wasn't gonna stop. It was a sense of terrible loneliness, when you desperately need someone, anyone to help you dig when the stakes are so high."

By now, the rescue team had been trying for hours to reach what they believed was David's position, and had found nothing there. At this point, Lassen Park Ranger Mike LaLone considered the mission more of a recovery than a rescue.

"People who are buried by avalanches don't survive much longer than about thirty minutes," he states. "It was pretty unlikely that Dennis was still alive."

Mike gave out the orders, and, not knowing that David and Dennis were still a half-mile away, the team decided to spread out on foot and search the area, leaving behind the snowcab they'd ridden up the mountain. Two hours later, they still hadn't found the men.

Dennis had now been buried for four hours.

"I was slowing down because I was losing strength, and I was beginning to feel hypothermia," explains David. "Time sort of lost its meaning. And quite frankly, I was beginning to panic. I wanted so much to find Dennis, to pull him out of there. I just prayed for those guys to reach us."

And then, he says, "I heard the crackling of a radio. And I thought it might be the trick of the wind, because that'd happened many times before."

But it was no trick. It was rescue volunteer Frank Ward, who had seen David's skis crossed in the snow.

"As I got closer, within maybe ten or fifteen feet, Dave popped his head up out of the hole he had dug," recalls Frank.

David was overcome with relief at the sight of Frank. "Inside of myself, something kind of let go, and I started to shake uncontrollably."

Frank radioed the other rescuers, who soon arrived. While they prepared to search for Dennis, David was taken back to the snowcab to get warm.

Meanwhile, Frank and the rescue team were trying to locate Dennis's body, using probes and a search dog.

"We put the dog on alert, and wherever the dog reacted, we began to probe," says Frank. "It was basically a first-response probe. You know, see what you can find."

But after several attempts, they'd found nothing.

"I was waiting in the snowcab, wondering what was next," remembers David. "It was like the avalanche hit me emotionally, right then, and it gave me permission to feel the full weight of the undeniable fact that Dennis must be dead. That my friend of twenty years died in front of my eyes."

It was more than four-and-a-half hours after Dennis was buried that rescuers finally arrived on the scene and began searching, and by now, they had given up all hope of finding the man alive.

Then, suddenly, Frank's probe hit something. The search dog confirmed the find, which appeared to be a glove. Still, Frank says, "I wasn't feeling real exhilarated at this point. We'd been out for like, what...five hours now? And the chance of finding a survivor at this point beats all the odds. But," he continues, "I felt like we had to keep moving. Against all odds."

"I didn't really wanna do it," Frank admits, "but I reached in and I grabbed the glove." Which, as he discovered, was still on Dennis's hand.

"The dog began to react very violently to the human scent," recalls Frank. "And at that point, somebody over my shoulder said, 'I hear moaning.' And I dove back down the hole, saying, 'Dennis, Dennis, are you with me?'"

"This simply shouldn't have happened," says Frank, amazed. "I just kept going, Yes, this is a good day."

The rescuers who were with Dennis radioed over to the rescuers who were with David in the snowcab, "We need some oxygen up here. We also need some more shovelers."

"And it took a moment to sink in," says David, "but I realized that Dennis must be alive, or they wouldn't need an oxygen bottle. And I whooped. I hit my head on the top of the snowcab. I couldn't believe it!"

Miraculously, after five-and-a-half hours buried under nearly six feet of snow, Dennis Eucalyptus was still alive.

On the way to the chalet where the ambulance awaited, David repeated over and over, "Dennis, it's David. It's David. Dennis, can you hear me? We're gonna be home soon." But as he recalls, "It took about forty-five minutes to reach the chalet. And all that time, Dennis didn't respond to us whatsoever."

"I was terribly worried he was gone," says Frank. "That his head, his mind, was gone."

Dennis was rushed to the hospital, where Dr. Dana Ware was standing by.

"I was concerned that he had been cold enough, and without oxygen long enough, to where he would have brain damage," concedes Dr. Ware. "But within about an hour of being in the emergency room, his body temperature went up to about 94 degrees. He was fairly coherent." Upon examination, Dr. Ware discovered, "He had absolutely no evidence of frostbite. I was absolutely astonished that he had survived so intact." She admits, "There is no scientific explanation. Science would have had him... well, dead and buried."

"I think what happened to him is a miracle," she says.

When David arrived back at the hospital a few hours later, he was relieved to find his friend awake and alert. "As soon as I entered, he turned to me and he smiled. And I said, 'Dennis, your middle name ought to be Lazarus from now on. You've come back from the grave.'"

Dennis sees it another way. "I took him by the shoulders and I said, 'David, if it wasn't for you, I wouldn't be alive.' I'm here today because David did exactly the right thing."

"I can't explain it any other way, but this was a miracle. That one of us survived to be able to get help. That is a miracle. That the phone worked, so that I could call for help. That is a miracle," says David. "The probe was only six feet long, and his hand was five-and-a-half feet under the surface. And that they found his hand in that avalanche field is astounding to me.

"I am just awed by the fact that God has touched us all in a very special way," he says.

The 22nd Annual Snow Madness trip went smoothly in February of 2001. And for Dennis, being able to return to the wilderness with his friend is the greatest miracle of all.

"David and I, we always felt we were somewhat brothers before," says Dennis of his relationship with David. "But now, having faced death in this way, I actually owe my life to David. I think that in some ways, that will bind us together in a way that we probably can't even articulate.

"I absolutely think that this was a bona fide miracle."

TWISTER SURVIVAL

When a violent tornado struck Nashville, Tennessee, without warning on May 18, 1995, it set in motion a series of incredible events that would change the lives of two complete strangers.

It was just after noon on a Thursday. Jan Neve was working her shift as office manager at Haverty's Furniture Store when she looked out to see the sky turning an eerie shade of green.

"I thought, Wow, I have never seen anything like this before," recalls Jan. "I stood there for a moment and then the lights went off."

The sky was rumbling loudly. A woman's scream brought

Jan running to the lunchroom door. She opened it to calm down whoever was inside, but just then, the twister touched down. The heavy door slammed shut on Jan's hand, crushing it, trapping her in place, and exposing her to the full force of the tornado.

Nearby, windows suddenly imploded.

"The entire building literally exploded around me. Glass was everywhere...there were huge pieces of glass," Jan remembers with horror. "The air-conditioning units were falling. Tons and tons of things were breaking and crashing. I said, 'I am not going to survive this.'"

The building was being ripped from its foundation, showering her with debris. But for Jan, there was no escape.

"I tried to pull that door," says Jan, "and I pulled and I pulled, but my hand was just stuck there. And finally I said, 'God, please help me.'"

And then, just as suddenly as this violent storm had appeared...it was gone.

"The sky turned blue. The storm had passed over," Jan recalls. "And I was able to finally pull that door open and off my hand, but there was not a lot left of my hand."

Jan sat down in the middle of the room, holding her hand and trying to dial the phone for help. She was bleeding profusely, and she knew that if she didn't get help, she could die. But the phones were dead. The store and the entire neighborhood around it had been reduced to rubble. Jan walked outside and looked around, but there wasn't a car or person in sight who could take her to a hospital.

"I could get no help and no help could get to me," Jan says, reliving the trauma. "So I thought, I'll just go and sit on the curb, and I'm going to bleed to death right here. This is the day that I'm going to die."

Jan was completely alone. Only a miracle could save her now.

Suddenly, out of nowhere, a pickup truck appeared. The driver, Robert Morgan, had had absolutely no intention of being in Nashville that day. But something mysterious had forced him to change course, guiding him on a path that led directly to the furniture store.

"I looked around," Robert says, "and I all I saw were downed poles and power lines all over these cars. And I thought, Man! You've got to get out of here. And all of a sudden, I looked around to my right and there comes Jan out to the door."

"Could you take me to the hospital?" Jan asked.

Robert was eager to help, but he wasn't from the Nashville area, and he had no idea where the nearest hospital was located. Jan, still suffering from shock, was forced to become the navigator.

They started to drive to the hospital. "Jan was saying, 'Please hurry,'" Robert recalls. "And for some reason I said, 'No, it's time to stop.'"

As Robert slammed on the brakes, a damaged live power line fell directly in front of them. A moment later, and they could have been electrocuted. Amazingly, there was still enough room for Robert and Jan to drive under the wire, but their day of terror wasn't over yet.

As lightning flashed and the sky rumbled, Jan and Robert drove on toward the hospital, all the while trying to stop Jan's bleeding. Jan's loss of blood had reached a critical stage. Robert struggled to remove his belt for her to use as a tourniquet while they sped through the tornado wreckage.

"Oh, please hurry," Jan cried. "I'm bleeding so much."

"Jan was bleeding real bad," confirms Robert. "And all I could think was She's going to pass out on me, and then where will I be? Because I didn't know where I was going."

In desperation, Robert used his cell phone to get directions to the hospital. But those directions led him straight back into the path of the tornado.

Robert describes the struggle to drive through the storm: "It was tearing up everything in its path. I could still feel the winds shaking the truck. I mean, it just felt like it was going to flip over anytime."

Suddenly, a section of roof filled with nails flew into the path of the truck. Robert braced himself for a blowout as the truck ran over the nails. But, miraculously, the tires weren't damaged. Robert and Jan sped on.

"The truck just seemed to be protected," Robert says, "like a big bowl was over the top of it, just moving along with us."

When they finally arrived at the hospital, Jan was rushed into surgery. Fearing the loss of her hand, she would encounter one last astonishing incident of good fortune.

Says Jan, "One of the nurses patted me on the shoulder, and she said, 'You know, this is your lucky day.' And the thought went through my mind, If *this* is my lucky day?...But the nurse said, 'Normally we don't have an orthopedic surgeon in surgery on Thursday.' "

And, in fact, the surgeon was able to save Jan's hand that afternoon. Today, Jan has almost completely recovered and has even been able to continue playing the piano. Both she and Robert are still amazed by the mysterious forces that brought them together that day.

"There are so many things that happened that day," says Robert, "it's hard for me to comprehend. I know that we were surrounded by a force...and it just protected us."

"My life was spared," agrees Jan, "due to a number of miracles that took place. There is no logical reason for my survival."

But there may be another explanation. Jan believes that Robert was sent to her as a guardian angel.

"I would not be here today if it wasn't for him," Jan says.

Robert, though, is humble. "If you ask the people I know...I'm no angel. I believe that our guardian angels were *both* there."

PINK PHOENIX

Early on the morning of March 25, 2000, a very special group of women assembled on the bank of the Willamette River in Portland, Oregon. They were there for dragon-boat racing.

But what made the Pink Phoenix Paddling Team so special was that each of them was a survivor of breast cancer.

As Karen Zwickert, who joined the team three years ago, says, "Pink Phoenix's goal really is to show the community how successful life can be after breast cancer."

Another survivor, Joan Cavanagh, became part of the team when she learned that joining a support group actually lowers the risk of cancer recurring.

"I'm not the type of person who wants to sit around and just listen to people talk about their diagnosis," says Joan. "I have a lot of energy, and so I wanted to be around other people who had a lot of energy."

Sharing laughter and tears, the members of the Pink Phoenix push each other to live life to its fullest.

For Linda Stafford, it was an important lesson. As she puts it, "I realize that life is too precious. So let's just get to the point of things and get them done, so we can get on with life and enjoy what there is out there."

But the morning's practice would drive home that lesson in a way that no one could have predicted.

"We got a kind of an unusual start," recalls Karen. "We didn't have enough paddlers to get on the boat and be able to get out there. Luckily, our team physician, Dr. Jeffery, was hanging around that morning."

"So we asked Dr. Jeffery to come with us," says Joan. "He hopped in, and Karen and I got in the front since we were the people who had the most experience."

As they headed out on the run, Linda took the position of "caller." It would be her job to keep the team's strokes in perfect rhythm.

"Out timing was terrible," Karen remembers. "It was really hard to get focused. Joan and I were the leads, but I had not been the lead previously, and Linda was our caller, but she hadn't done much calling before."

"Think about doing that as you're paddling," remarks Linda.

"So we were definitely out of sync that morning, no question about it," says Karen.

"We're just more about having fun, we didn't really look at it as a practice where we have to learn something. So we determined we'd stay a little closer to the marina than we usually do," recalls Linda. "We're never where we were, at that time of the morning."

And if they hadn't been there, the miracle that was about to happen might never have occurred.

"As we were paddling, I saw something fall from the bridge," says Karen. "Something red caught my eye, and I said to Joan, 'Joan, is that a person?'"

"There's a moment of disbelief while you're trying to let it sink in, you know, that that just doesn't happen," Linda says. "This is a tall bridge, and people don't just fall off bridges."

The team quickly moved into action, paddling furiously toward the bridge.

"There was no time to sit and talk about whether we should go or not. We just went," states Joan. "There was so much energy on that boat. We were flying across the water."

And suddenly, their paddles fell into sync, striking the water with perfect precision and force.

"It was like everyone was right on target," recalls Karen. "We paddled so fast, so well—like one blade, like we're supposed to do—in getting over there. I think about half to three quarters of the way across the river, we could actually see that it was a person. He was wearing a red parka, it looked like it was down, and it sort of buoyed him up, almost like a life jacket. But then as we got closer, I could see that the jacket had kind of filled with water and was starting to pull him down."

By the time the Pink Phoenix team reached the man in the red parka, he was barely conscious.

"Karen and Joan reached out and tried to pull him in, and then held on to him," says Linda.

"We didn't know what we were gonna do, because the boat is so narrow in front," clarifies Joan. "There wasn't much we could do to pull him into the boat."

But if they didn't get him out of the water quickly, the freezing temperature would surely kill him.

"That's a very cold river. Survival in the Willamette in March probably is just minutes," affirms Linda.

"Somebody yelled that there was a fishing boat that was coming down toward us," says Joan. "And we held him up until they got there."

The fishermen helped pull the young man out of the water and onto their boat, and everyone prayed that he would live, not knowing the full extent of his injuries.

"We didn't know at that time what kind of damage might have been done to his spine or any other bones," says Linda. "And Dr. Jeffery was able to tell as soon as he got up there and checked his pulse. He said, 'Yeah, he's still got a strong pulse. Somebody throw me something warm.'"

The doctor was still concerned that the young man might be suffering from hypothermia, but as Linda says, "We didn't have any blankets or anything. But we all had jackets on, so people started stripping off their jackets and handing them to Dr. Jeffery to cover the man with. It's not much, but it keeps the wind off."

The boat raced toward shore with the young man clinging to life. It was only then that the women of the Pink Phoenix realized the importance of what had just happened.

"I think we were all still in shock. I know I was," Linda admits. "It's kind of like, Oh, well, we just pulled somebody out of the river."

"Everybody all of a sudden went, Oh, my God," recalls Karen. Once they realized the magnitude of what they had just done, the women began to congratulate one another—but there was also an undercurrent of something else.

"Many of the women talked about how they had striven to be alive, because of their breast cancer experience," reveals Karen. "And thinking that perhaps this person didn't *want* to live was just a real dichotomy for them. A real difficult thing."

Once on shore, an ambulance with an emergency medical team moved in to take control of the situation. As the young man was placed into the ambulance, the women couldn't help but wonder if they would ever again meet the man they'd just saved.

"For days after, I wondered about him," says Joan. "I was really glad to see his name in the paper on Sunday, because he had a name then."

The women learned that the man's name was Dale Buttenhoff, and that he had been taken to Oregon Health & Science University.

"Linda and I talked for a long time about what we

should do," Joan remembers. "Because we were just very worried about him. We wanted to make sure he was okay."

"You don't really know whether this person's going to be glad to see you or not," agrees Linda. "You know, maybe they didn't want to be rescued and you ruined it for them."

But fortunately, Dale realized that these ladies had given him a second chance to set his life right. He welcomed their visit warmly; and for their part, the women came laden with gifts.

"They showed up with flowers, cards, balloons," says Dale, "and said how nice it was to see me, under better circumstances."

"Everyone on the boat wants you to come down. We're going to take you for a ride as soon as you're well," Joan told him.

"He was very friendly, and very open, and very appreciative," she recalls. "He was really happy to see us, and that made us feel good."

As the women gained Dale's trust, he told them what had actually happened on the bridge that fateful day.

On March 25, 2000, Dale Buttenhoff was at the lowest point in his life when he began climbing high above the Willamette River. Dale had been battling a drug addiction that left him alienated from his entire family.

"I had come to a point in my life where I just wasn't real happy with what was going on, and I just didn't like myself very much," confesses Dale. "There was just, I guess, just sadness left at what my life had become."

What weighed most heavily on Dale's mind was his daughter, whom he hadn't seen much of since his divorce.

"My daughter was about two years old—she's the best thing that ever happened to me, and I was feeling like I let her down. I just wasn't there for her," Dale says. "The way I was living my life, I knew I wouldn't be there for her anyway. So I was kind of taking the easy way out," he reflects.

Dale had planned his suicide for weeks. In fact, in order not to embarrass his family, he had stayed clean and sober for twenty days and even bought a new set of clothes.

"I didn't want to be known as Dale, this druggie who took his life. I wanted to be clean. You know, I wanted people to think that I was in the right state of mind," he explains.

And at that point, his mind was made up.

"I don't even know what got my legs to just give me that little push to go up and over," Dale says, "but once I did, I knew that I hadn't done the right thing. At the same time, there's no turning back. I'm over."

Amazingly, it was his new red jacket that kept Dale afloat and that caught the attention of the Pink Phoenix team.

"The last thing I remember is the voices," says Dale. "I remember all these voices around me, and I remember them pulling me up on something flat. The words 'I'm sorry' were coming out of my mouth, and it was like I said, saying sorry for everything. I was saying sorry to my daughter. Sorry to my parents. Sorry to my sisters and family and sorry to these ladies."

But the ladies of the Pink Phoenix didn't need an apology. Many of them were mothers themselves and what they were feeling wasn't anger but sadness.

"I thought to myself, He looks like he's very close in age to my sons," recalls Joan. "Your children are so precious; and this was somebody's child. And I thought about what his mom would feel like when she heard that he had gone off the bridge. What a worry that would be for a mom."

It was these maternal feelings that brought Joan and Linda to the hospital, along with some very special gifts.

"I took him a Bible, and I took him a picture frame, and tulips," says Linda. "The picture frame, because I told him that I wanted him to put a picture of his daughter in it. And the tulips are very meaningful to me, because back when I planted them I said, 'I don't even know if I'm gonna be here in the spring to see them come up.' And I was. And now my yard's full of tulips, and to me they're really a sign of renewal."

And thanks to the miracle that saved him, Dale's life is also experiencing a renewal. He's been given a second chance to be a loving father to his young daughter.

"The relationship with my daughter is turned around 110 percent. I've made a commitment to myself and to her that I'm not going to let the past ruin what kind of relationship my daughter and I can have," Dale says. "She's always been there for me. I made now a commitment to be there for her."

The ladies of Pink Phoenix still keep in touch with Dale and his family, and in turn, they've acquired a new fan. Dale now regularly attends the dragon-boat races.

"Dale now has forty-eight mothers in addition to his own," declares Joan. "Everyone on the team is very supportive of him, and knows him, and has absolutely fallen for him. So he really has to live up to the expectation of forty-eight mothers in addition to his own."

And his own mother, Georgia Mansfield, agrees.

"The ladies have really kept him on the straight and narrow. They said, 'If you need us to come over and give him a kick in the butt and get him going in the right direction, we'll come over and do that,'" she says. "They were real people that really cared about other people. I pray for their health and their happiness every day of my life, because they gave me back something so precious to me."

Dale is a living testament to the courage and determination of the Pink Phoenix team. Each of them has survived her own brush with death, and together, they defied death once again in saving Dale Buttenhoff's life. For all of them, it was nothing less than a miracle.

"The circumstances that morning were amazing. The fact that we even saw Dale go off the bridge was amazing. And then we crossed that river at an incredibly fast rate of speed," says Joan.

"We were at the right place at the right time," she adds, "and somebody sent us there. I don't ever think those things happen without a purpose, and without some intervention. Some divine intervention."

THE GIFT OF LIFE

DANNY'S WISH

Kathleen and John Carlsen were married in 1975. They both came from large families and hoped to have one of their own. But, sadly, that was not meant to be.

"We had a very, very difficult time," John recalls. "We had been married eight years, and Kathleen had many miscarriages before she finally became pregnant. We were overjoyed at the fact that we were going to have a child... and then sometime after the first three months, we went for a routine ultrasound."

"And on that ultrasound," says Kathleen, "they picked up a birth defect called hydrocephalus, which is water on the brain. And we were told that the life expectancy of a child with hydrocephalus is not very promising."

"We were completely, completely floored. Many of the specialists we had seen and talked to were urging us to end the pregnancy," recalls John, but Kathleen was not comfortable with that.

"We just decided to go ahead with having the baby," she says. "We just felt that there must be a reason for this pregnancy to be holding on."

Four months later, Kathleen gave birth to a premature baby boy whom they named Danny. But tragically, Danny suffered from more than just hydrocephalus.

"Danny had something called spina bifida," explains John. "It's a birth defect that causes a malformation of the spine. If Danny survived through the night, and if he survived after that, he would never walk, he would never say 'Mama,' and he'd probably be retarded."

The Carlsens were not ready to accept that prognosis. "It made me feel very, very angry because you just kinda say, 'Wait a second. How can you predict that? Nobody can predict the future,'" says Kathleen. "The first twenty-four to forty-eight hours were very critical. And he was so tiny . . . just so tiny," she recalls with tears in her eyes. "But I reached my hand into his bassinet and I touched him and I told him I was there. And then we just waited."

Danny did survive, and four weeks later, the Carlsens took their son home, knowing that he would face a lifetime of medical problems.

"Most of his body functions from his head to his toes were impaired in some way," says John. "We decided that we were just going to love him and take care of him and do the best we could. He was our pride and joy, even if he wasn't perfect."

As Kathleen points out, "Danny's development was a little bit delayed, but not so bad that you would say, 'Oh, my gosh, that child is very delayed.' I remember going to the pediatrician when Danny was eighteen months and saying, 'He's not babbling; he's not doing the baby talk.' The doctor said, 'Well, if he doesn't talk by two, then we'll have a problem.'" And in fact, she recalls, "Just around the time Danny turned two, he started talking. He really didn't do any baby talk. He just came right out with sentences."

From the beginning, Danny possessed a love for life that couldn't be dampened.

"He was an inspiration to a lot of people who would look at him and say, 'How can he be so upbeat, so happy, in the face of everything that he deals with on a daily basis?'" says John. "Through the years, he continued to have a lot of surgeries. He had to wear a brace on his body, braces on his legs. He walked with crutches at first, and eventually he had to use a wheelchair. But he was a fighter and he didn't seem to realize that he had these disabilities or these handicaps at all. We were incredibly proud of this kid."

And Danny was incredibly proud of his father.

"I've been a member of the police department for more than twenty-eight years now. And Danny thought cops were the greatest people in the world," says John fondly.

Kathleen, too, recalls taking Danny's scout troop over to the precinct periodically to go on tours. "And then he would really be, 'This is my dad's police department.' It wasn't the Nassau County Police Department, it was his *dad's* police department."

Like so many other officers at John's precinct, Larry Gilrain became attached to this courageous young man.

"When Danny used to show up at the precinct," he says, "if I was having a down day, Danny was the type of person who would always bring you up. He always had a grin on his face no matter how much pain he was in, and I know the pain at times was excruciating. But Danny always remained upbeat," Larry recalls. "In his mind there was still hope that he was gonna one day be a police officer and make himself, and his father, proud."

"He desperately wanted to be a police officer when he grew up," John agrees. "He had his own uniforms. He had his own police scanner." Home videos capture the moment when Danny received the scanner, as well as John telling his son, "You're going to get to listen to all the calls that Daddy gets on his radio," and Danny's excited reply, "Oh, my God!"

Of Danny's love for the police, John recalls, "He lived it. He loved it. It was his life. I knew, of course, with the disabilities he had he just couldn't do it. But I never had the heart to tell him that. I just couldn't tell him that."

But no one could protect twelve-year-old Danny Carlsen from what was about to happen to him. On August 15, 1995, Danny suddenly stopped breathing.

"We were in his bedroom with him and I pulled him down on the floor and started to do CPR," says John. "And I told Kathy to call 911 and tell them that he was in full cardiac arrest and that we needed someone here right away." The police arrived soon after. "The very cops he loved and knew took over and started to work on him."

"The next thing I know, the officers come in, and they tell me to get out. And I basically knew at that time that my baby was no longer with me," sobs Kathleen.

Danny was rushed to the hospital, where he was diagnosed with a severe viral infection.

"I walked in and I held his hand and I said, 'Come on, Danny, you gotta pull through, you gotta do this,'" says John. Amazingly, the heart monitor started to beep—but not for very long. "And for one brief moment, we saw heartbeats on the monitor...and then there weren't any more." He pauses. "And I had lost the light of my life."

"I just was, like, 'My baby, where did he go?'" cries Kathleen. "It was really the worst day of my life."

With Danny's death, John and Kathleen were left to make one of the most difficult decisions of their lives.

"Kathy volunteered the suggestion that we donate whatever organs they could take. Because of the condition of his body, the only thing that they were willing to take was his corneas. So they took both of his eyes, which were donated later to people who needed to have cornea transplants."

In an extraordinary tribute, the police gave Danny a funeral normally reserved for fallen officers.

"This was the way that they could show him and the rest of the world how much they really cared for this boy," says John. "They had arranged to have police cars, emergency services trucks, even a bagpipe. I don't know if I've ever seen anything like this before. I was overwhelmed. And I knew it was what Danny would have wanted."

Adds Kathleen, "Over a thousand people came to Danny's funeral. The lines at the funeral home were out the door and down the block."

A month after Danny's death, John felt compelled to write an important letter.

"We decided that we'd like to know who got Danny's corneas," he says, then admits, "What we really wanted to do was to tell them about this child."

I'd like you to know a little bit about him so you might be able to appreciate the gift you received. Danny was twelve years old. He died suddenly, unexpectedly . . .

John's letter reached thirty-two-year-old Ray Mareno, who had nearly lost his eyesight in a freak accident. "When I was on vacation in the Dominican Republic," Ray explains, "I had taken my contact lens out of my right eye. It caught up on the top part of my eye and ripped my cornea. The doctor had told me I would be losing sight in my right eye if I didn't go and get a cornea transplant."

It was Danny's cornea that would perform the miracle that would restore Ray's sight.

"When I was called in for the transplant, I was very excited that I would be able to see out of my right eye again," says Ray. But the miracle didn't end there. "It was a very successful operation. And I was soon back to full duty, very glad, and continued my career."

His career?...Ray Mareno is a police officer.

After Ray read John's letter, he was struck by the coincidences. "I was amazed to see that John was a police officer. I was a police officer. Their son Danny wanted to become a police officer." Ray decided that he wanted to meet the Carlsens. "I wanted to share my story with them, as they did with me."

"He told us that he was a city police officer and had received the cornea transplant a few days after Danny died, and that it had saved his job," says John in amazement. "I believe that this truly was a miracle. I believe that God was at work here."

"We were just so excited that Danny finally got to live his dream. He couldn't be a police officer physically here, but he's helping a police officer do his job," asserts Kathleen.

"I live in John's precinct, and when I walk out in the morning, you could say that Danny looks out over his dad's precinct just like he used to," says Ray.

Declares John, "Is that a miracle? There's no doubt in my mind."

BABY SISTER MIRACLE

It was 1988 and Anissa Ayala had just celebrated her sixteenth birthday when she was diagnosed with leukemia, a deadly form of cancer. The news came as an emotional blow to Anissa's parents, Mary and Abe Ayala.

"When I heard 'leukemia,'" recalls Abe, "to me it was a death sentence. It devastated me. I knew I was going to lose her."

"I remember I started crying," says Mary, "and I said, 'Well, what's going to happen to her? Where do we go or what do we do?'"

In a sobering meeting with their doctor, the Ayalas learned that Anissa's only chance for survival was a bone marrow transplant.

When Anissa asked what would happen if she didn't get the transplant, Mary says, "He just came out and told us, 'She's gonna die.' That's all there is to it."

Anissa's parents did their best to comfort her, and assure her that they'd find a donor. The best chance of finding a suitable donor was within the Ayala family, but after extensive testing, no matches were found. And so, they turned to the National Marrow Donor Program.

"There were only 17,000 in the registry, and they told us that her chances were only one in 20,000," says Abe. "So the odds were just all against us at that time."

"Immediately, we started working on trying to find a donor, campaigning throughout the community and asking for help," says Mary. "We didn't have time to feel sorry for ourselves. We were just too busy trying to recruit donors into the registry."

But months passed without finding a matching donor. And then a family friend suggested a radical solution: Mary and Abe should have another child...and perhaps this one would match.

"She planted that seed in my head, that maybe it could be possible," recalls Mary. "When I talked to Abe about it, he said, 'You're nuts. We can't do that.'"

And even if they wanted to, Abe had undergone a vasectomy shortly after Anissa's birth, which would require reversal surgery.

The chance of a vasectomy reversal leading to pregnancy was 50 percent. The chance of a forty-two-year-old woman conceiving was 73 percent. The chance of blood-related siblings being a perfect match was just 25 percent. And the chance of a bone marrow transplant curing leukemia was 70 percent.

All in all, the odds were only 6.4 percent.

But Mary refused to give up.

"I was really adamant in my heart about doing this," states Mary, "and Abe was always saying, 'Well, wait a little longer, wait a little bit longer.' But time, for Anissa, was of the essence."

And then, one night, any doubts the Ayalas may have had were erased by a dream.

"I saw a family scene, and I saw Anissa, and I saw a baby there," recalls Mary, "and then all of a sudden a voice started talking to me, saying, 'Go ahead and have another child, everything is going to work out.' I woke up so startled, my heart was pounding. I woke Abe up and I told him, 'Abe, God is telling me that this is what we have to do.'

"I really believe this was a sign from God," she declares.

"Something was assuring us that we should do this," agrees Abe. "And everything, everything just fell into place from then on."

Within weeks, Abe underwent surgery to reverse his vasectomy, and four months later, Mary was pregnant. The odds were getting better.

"We were just really confident that God wouldn't bring us this far without going all the way," says Mary.

Seven months into her pregnancy, Mary was given an amniocentesis test. The results were the miracle they'd been waiting for.

Abe and Mary told Anissa the good news, saying, "We

talked to the doctor today. You're going to have a baby sister . . . and that's not all. She's a perfect match."

On April 3, 1990, Mary gave birth to a healthy baby girl—Marissa Eve.

"It's a part of my name and a part of Anissa's name," explains Mary. "And I read that Eve meant 'The Life-Giving One,' so that's why we named her Eve."

But Anissa's life was still in danger. Her doctors would not be able to perform the bone marrow transplant until the baby was at least fourteen months old.

"She was so tiny, she didn't weigh enough to be a donor," recalls Abe. "By then, you could say that we were racing against time."

"I think that it kept Anissa so strong, to know that she had to survive this in order to see her little sister grow up," says Mary.

"Finally, when Marissa was big enough," says Abe, "with a combination of her marrow and umbilical cord stem cells, they had enough for the transplant."

The delicate operation was scheduled for June 4, 1991, at City of Hope Hospital in Los Angeles. Anissa was admitted two weeks prior to the surgery, during which time she endured massive doses of chemotherapy and radiation to prepare her body to accept the new marrow.

"They kill you off," says Abe, "and then machines keep you alive, and then that's when they put the marrow in through the IV. And then the battle starts.

"The doctor was honest when he told us right up front that it was a fifty-fifty chance," admits Abe, adding, "I don't like them odds."

But Anissa survived the transplant, beating the odds once again. For the next thirty days, she would recover in the hospital, isolated, while her body adapted to the new marrow.

"No children were allowed on the ward at all, so the only way I was ever able to see my sister was through a glass window," recalls Anissa. "I just hoped and I prayed that I'd be able to walk outside and be able to thank my sister for what she had done."

Anissa's prayer was answered on July 5, 1991, when she finally returned home.

"We got a few of her friends and family together, and everyone had masks on and they had balloons...it was so great to have her home," says Mary. "To know that she actually had made it. She had made it."

More than eleven years have passed since Anissa's transplant, and at the five-year mark, she was officially considered cancer-free.

She continues to have a very close relationship with her family, especially with her little sister, Marissa, who is now twelve years old.

"The bond between her and me is just incredible," Anissa reveals. "It's like she's a daughter to me. And through all the radiation and chemo I've been through, they don't know if I'm able to have children. So right now, I'm satisfied with her.

"I really believe that the Lord has guided us in this whole situation," she adds. "There were just too many things that were against us—my mother's age, my father's reversing a seventeen-year-old vasectomy, the odds of the child being a match—it's really been incredible, and it's been a blessing for everyone, because my sister is such a sweetheart. She's such a wonderful little angel that really God has given us."

SHAFEEQ'S GIFT

Like other fifteen-year-olds, Shafeeq Murrell had dreams: to get his driver's license, to go to college, maybe even to play in the NBA. But life wasn't always so easy for Shafeeq. He was born severely premature, and doctors had warned his mother, Gail, that he might not live.

"Shafeeq weighed only two pounds at birth," Gail recalls. "But when he came out, his lungs were fully developed. He didn't have any heart problems. His brain was fully developed, and the only thing he had to do was stay in the hospital and gain weight.

"He was a miracle baby," she says. "He was a blessing. He was my pride and joy."

Stacey Murrell, Shafeeq's sister, was especially fond of her little brother.

"He was just the type of kid that people liked to be around," she says. "When you said Shafeeq's name, everyone's face just kind of lit up. It was a good thing."

"He knew at a young age that he had to work to get things in life that he wanted," Gail says. "He loved to work, and he did exceptionally well."

Even Ingrid Burnett, the supervisor on Shafeeq's after-school job, could see the incredible potential in this young man.

"Shafeeq was probably one of the most mature young men of fifteen," says Ingrid. "Every day he walked me down in the subway to the booth, and said good night after I paid. He said, 'I just want to make sure that nobody doesn't mug you or hurt you or anything like that.' I found that kind of fascinating, for a fifteen-year-old to think of something like that without anyone saying it."

But on February 28, all of Shafeeq's hopes and dreams were taken away by a random act of violence, when he was caught in the crossfire between two rival gang members.

Shafeeq's mother was just returning home when she received the terrifying news.

"I couldn't believe it," Gail says. "I hadn't even taken off my coat when a young lady, who lived across the street at the time, said, 'Miss Gail, Miss Gail, come! They shot Shafeeq! They shot Shafeeq!'"

Gail immediately ran to where Shafeeq had been shot. "It took me forever just to run those two blocks. And there

Shafeeq lay on the ground, and he had this big hole in his head. He was just laying there, just looking in a daze. And I was just rubbing his head, saying, 'Shafeeq, you're going to be okay. Just stay with us, just a little bit, you're going to be okay.'"

The dying boy was rushed to Children's Hospital. His sister, Stacey, frantically made her way there as soon as she heard about the shooting.

"I go over to the bed, and I look at him," she recalls. "And I know that he's gone. But my mother says, 'He's gonna be okay. He's going to wake up. He's going to be fine.'"

Stacey says, "I didn't have the heart to tell her that he's not okay."

"It was just horrible, just watching him and not being able to do anything for him at all," remembers Gail. "All I knew is, I wanted Shafeeq just to live, to be able just to live. I just didn't want him to die."

The family stayed by Shafeeq's side in the hospital and prayed. "When the doctors came into the room and said that there was nothing else left for them to do to bring Shafeeq back, a sense of relief came over me," says Stacey, "because I didn't know how much longer I could go on pretending like he was coming back. And at the same time," she says, "my entire world crashed."

There was nothing left to do but to remove Shafeeq from life support.

"There were nurses who came to us and asked about organ and tissue donation," says Gail. "I kind of went off and said, why, no, I *didn't* want to donate his organs and things like that. But then, something just came over me. It was for Shafeeq to give back, because he was a miracle baby.

"That miracle was given to me by God," explains Gail. "So it was my turn to give that miracle back, so that somebody else can have a miracle in their life."

"After we said yes to tissue and organ donation," says Stacey, "then the doctors came back into the room and told us it was time to say our final good-byes."

"And he just lay there. Just like he was sleeping. Like he was going to sleep for the night," she recalls.

"That was so hard, saying good-bye to him," says Gail. "So hard to say good-bye to him."

Across town at Temple University Hospital, another tragedy had been unfolding. Larry Montgomery, a thirty-nine-year-old dentist and father of three, was on the brink of death from a genetic heart disease.

Larry's only hope was a heart transplant.

His wife, Sheree, tried to keep up a brave front, but her own heart was filled with fear.

"Inside my mind I constantly had thoughts of losing Larry, and having to deal with helping the children to live through that," Sheree says. "Looking at Larry being so sick, I knew that he couldn't last much longer. But weeks would go by, with no hearts available."

At long last, a heart unexpectedly became available late one night.

"I was quite surprised," says Larry. "When I called my wife she thought I was joking, because of my sense of humor.

"But I said, 'No, you need to get down here right away.'"

His family rushed to the hospital to be with him. "When we said good-bye," recalls Larry, "we all held hands, and we said a prayer for the donor family and the donor. We wanted to offer a prayer of thanks for the generosity of that donor family, who had to make a decision to donate those organs at probably the worst moment of their lives."

As Larry was taken into surgery, Sheree broke down. "They wheeled him into the operating room," she says, "and I was left there, just crying, because of a sudden realization that maybe I wouldn't see him again."

But the transplant surgery was successful. And after a few weeks recuperating, Larry returned home.

It was there that he began to wonder who had given him back his life.

"Initially, I didn't have thoughts about where the heart came from," admits Larry, "until my brother, who's a doctor, found out that it was a fifteen-year-old's heart, and that it had come from Children's Hospital.

"Sheree's sister heard the news reports, because Shafeeq's was a well-publicized death. It was on the local television stations. She clipped some of the articles out and gave them to Sheree, thinking this could possibly be my donor.

"And about two or three months after my transplant, I opened the envelope and read the articles."

The clues revealed that the heart beating inside Larry's chest might well be Shafeeq Murrell's.

"We suspected that he might be the donor. But we didn't know for sure," says Larry.

He felt compelled to write the donor family a letter.

"I would think almost every day about what I would say in that letter, but I just couldn't think of the right words," he says. "It took me ten months from the transplant to write that letter."

Early in the morning of March 2, 1996, you gave me a gift—the gift of a new life. And now I carry the heart of your loved one. This steady heartbeat is a reminder of you and your loss, and, fortunately, your loss has enabled me to move on. You are in my prayers every day.

"When I read the letter, I cried," says Gail. "And I read it again and I got very angry. I said, 'Who is this person to write me this letter, and tell me that I had to lose something in order for him to gain something?' When I read the letter and found out that the family wanted to meet me," she adds, "I wasn't ready. I wasn't ready."

Gail's refusal to meet Larry left him sad and depressed. But a miraculous set of events would soon bring him closer to the boy who'd saved his life.

Larry moved on with his life, taking a job teaching at a local university. It was there that he befriended a parking lot attendant.

"He would often ask me how I was feeling," says Larry. "He knew that I had had a heart transplant."

He adds, "He also admired my car, which was an older Cadillac. He kept asking me if I ever wanted to sell it, and one day I told him, 'It's for sale. Make me an offer.' He said to me, 'I'll give you $2,000 for it,' and I said, 'It's sold.'"

But before he could take legal possession of the vehicle, the buyer needed to retrieve his old license plates, and so Larry offered to drive him home.

"He proceeded to drive into South Philadelphia to his home," recalls Larry. "I looked around, and I thought, What am I doing? I'm in a strange neighborhood with $2,000 cash in my pocket. Why am I here?"

And that was when they crossed Wharton Street, which Larry suddenly remembered from the newspaper articles he'd read.

"I happened to mention to him, 'I think my donor lived on this street,'" says Larry. "And he said, 'What was his name?' And I said, 'Shafeeq Murrell.'"

"Shafeeq?" the man repeated.

"You know him?" Larry said.

"Yeah, I do. Yeah," he replied.

"Come on," Larry rejoined.

"My wife was his supervisor," he said.

"Are you serious?" Larry said.

"And I had goose bumps," says Larry. "I mean, it was a very strange, strange experience. And he said to me, 'Would you do me a favor? My wife worked very closely with Shafeeq, and was very close to this boy. Would you go to that phone right there and call her at work and tell her what you told me?'"

Larry agreed, and he introduced himself to Ingrid over the phone. "I'm the gentleman that's selling your husband the car," he said, then added, "I am a transplant recipient. I believe I have Shafeeq Murrell's heart."

"I was just so amazed," recalls Ingrid. "I felt as though I wanted to reach through the phone, because it felt like a part of Shafeeq maybe was on the other end of the phone. And I wanted to tell him that he had the heart of a very good person," she says. "Then I asked him if he had ever met Shafeeq's parents, and he said no, he hadn't. And I said to him, 'I think they may want to meet you.'"

Thanks to Ingrid and the remarkable coincidence, the identity of Larry's heart donor was finally confirmed. And the Murrells finally felt the time was right to meet the Montgomerys.

The first thing that Gail asked upon meeting Larry was whether she could feel Shafeeq's heart. Larry agreed.

"When I touched Larry's heart, I said, 'You have a good, strong heart here.' And we just both smiled at each other. Like, it was meant to be," Gail says. "So I was satisfied. I was happy. I was happy. Yeah, I was happy."

"When I first saw Larry standing there, I saw my brother standing there," remembers Stacey. "He is tall like Shafeeq; he's very sweet and kind like Shafeeq was. He knows how to say the right thing at the right moment, just like Shafeeq would. So, it's absolutely amazing to me how closely Larry and Shafeeq are matched."

Stacey declares, "I know that Shafeeq's heart found a wonderful home. I know that Shafeeq's heart is being very well taken care of. I know that Shafeeq's heart is going to be around for a long time."

"I think we were destined to meet. I think the sale of this car is what pushed us on it," says Larry. "I do think that it was a miracle that all this occurred, and that I was able to meet this family and thank them in person." Larry even gave them the bronze medal that he won in the U.S. Transplant Games.

"I call Larry and his family my second family. It was a match made in heaven," says Gail. "I think it's a wonderful legacy that Shafeeq has continued to live on in someone else's life. It was possible to turn a tragedy into a miracle."

KIDNEY ON TAP

Fifty-three-year-old Terry Buckwalter always dreamed of becoming a baseball coach, but in 1980, he bought a neighborhood bar—The Belgrade—in Moline, Illinois. And over the next twenty years, Terry traded in his dream for a thriving business.

"I never realized I'd become a bar owner," says Terry. "But it just happened, and it turned out it happened to be a good thing. There are a lot of people up there that are really good friends. In fact, most of my closest friends now come from my clientele."

But even Terry's closest friends didn't know the terrible secret he was hiding. His kidneys were slowly failing.

His wife, Kathy, watched helplessly as his condition continued to deteriorate.

"He just started progressively getting sicker," recalls Kathy. "He couldn't sleep, and he wouldn't eat right. And he would come home from work exhausted all the time and try to sleep, but get up and not sleep. He had been sick for almost the whole time we'd been married, and his kidneys were just deciding after twenty-odd years to give out. So I said, 'You need to do something.'"

Terry turned to dialysis treatments to stay alive. But his doctor, V. R. Alla, knew it was only a temporary measure... until a donor kidney could be found.

"If he does not receive the dialysis treatment," explains Dr. Alla, "the poisons will increase in his system, and eventually, he will go into a coma and die. It was very difficult for him to accept, and he'd get emotional ups and downs."

"Some people's bodies can take it, some can't," says Terry, "and I was the one who couldn't take it toward the end. And so I knew that I didn't have much longer, because you can't go on like that."

"It's hard to see somebody that you care about attached to a machine that's chugging, chugging," adds Kathy, "and you think it could be any minute, even attached to the machine, that he may not make it through. If his blood pressure goes too low, he could die, even on the dialysis machine. There was the sense of impending doom—it's keeping you alive, but your life's not good. It was terrible."

Eventually, it became impossible for Terry to hide his illness from his friends at the bar.

Friend Tracy Griffin says, "People were worried about him. I mean, he'd come in and he would just, you know, have no energy. He just looked bad. He was losing weight. He looked very bad."

Another friend, Brian Polson, adds, "It just...to be honest, most of the time I expected him not to be here the next day."

Terry's days were numbered. His only hope was a new kidney.

"Of course," Terry says, "my kids offered to give me their kidneys, but I just did not like that idea because I knew that the kind of disease I had is hereditary. And I would feel real bad if they gave me one of their kidneys and then down the road acquired the disease that I had. And I just couldn't live with that. So I was prepared just to wait for a cadaver."

But the wait for a suitable organ could take years... and so, one night at the bar, Terry made an unusual offer.

"Hey, guess what, guys," announced Terry, "anyone want to give me a kidney? They can drink free for the rest of their lives." He then added, "That's just a joke now."

Terry remembers, "Everybody started laughing, and I started laughing too."

But one man in the crowd wasn't laughing. Dee Pollard was too concerned.

"That's when the thought process started," explains Dee, "of what I could do, or what else could be done. So I approached Terry and asked him what he was going to do. And he said, 'What can I do, you know? I gotta wait.'"

"And Dee says, 'I'll give you one of my kidneys,'" adds Terry. "He said, 'I'd like to do that for you.' It was just out of the blue. I mean, I was shocked that here's a guy, a guy that knew me—but not that well—who would do something like that."

The next day, Terry approached Dee again, just to make sure he'd heard him right.

"I said, 'Were you really serious about giving me a kidney?' And he said, 'I'm prepared to do that. I want to do that,'" Terry recalls.

"What's your blood type?" Terry asked.

"My blood type is O-positive," replied Dee.

"Well, that's the first step," said Terry. "Because I'm O-positive." He admits, "Well, I knew it was still a long way from being a match, so my hopes were up, but they weren't up that much because anything can happen."

Not everyone was happy with Dee's decision—especially his sister, Garianne Gamble.

"I first heard it through my mother," says Garianne. "I didn't hear through Dee, and I didn't like it. And I'm sure he didn't tell me because he knew I wouldn't like it. Naturally, the first thing that went through my mind was 'Does he need the kidney because of the bar, because he'd been drinking?' You know, what's the problem here? But Dee told me that it wasn't from drinking, it wasn't from abusing his body, it was just that Terry had been ill for several years with a kidney disease.

"I asked him, 'What makes you feel that you need to be the one to do this?' And he said that he just felt in his heart that this was the thing he should do. He had some spiritual feeling that he was called to do this."

And so Dee Pollard began the series of tests that would seal Terry Buckwalter's fate.

"So after he took the first two or three tests," says Terry, "he came back and he said that the doctors were encouraged, that everything was going well. Then I started thinking, 'Well, God, maybe this is my angel.'"

"For the tissue match," Dee explains, "they went with the antigens, and out of six antigens, mine matched for four out of six. Which made it more like a relative's kidney."

"So Dee came in and said, 'Well, they called me. They want to do the operation in about two weeks,'" recalls Terry. "And it sort of shocked me. I said, 'Two weeks?' I said, 'Wow!'"

The operation was scheduled for November 6, 1998. It would be a first—the first time in Iowa that a living black donor would give an organ to a white recipient.

"I assumed that two races wouldn't necessarily mix," admits Kathy. "That's not true. Your kidney is your kidney, and it's pink, pink, pink. Whether you're yellow or black or white or red, it's pink!"

The seven-hour operation was even more successful than anyone had anticipated.

"The first thing they do when they come out of the anesthesia," recounts Kathy, "is they each ask about the other one."

"I was anxious to find out what happened, you know, during Terry's surgery," explains Dee. "When Dr. Ray Hill came into the room and said that the surgery was successful, that when they put my kidney in him it started pumping right away, I just thanked God right then and there."

"And they couldn't believe how fast it was working," adds Kathy. "His color came back, he was sitting up in bed. They didn't put Dee and Terry in the same room together, they were across the hall from each other. So you'd see these two guys in their hospital garb shuffling across their rooms, asking, 'How do you feel?' and the other one would say, 'Fine.' And then they'd go back and the other one would shuffle across the hall. You could watch the little flap in the back giving the nurses a thrill, keeping them on their toes, but it was great. It was great."

Garianne agrees, "The fact that the kidney started working right away, faster than they said any other one ever had, it was amazing, just amazing. I think that's the biggest thing. And the second biggest thing would be the way the community reacted."

"When we got back to the bar together," says Dee, "and everybody was there, they were very congratulatory, you know, a lot of high fives. I couldn't swing them because my side hurt, so there were a lot of low fives on my end."

Since the operation, Terry has returned to his old self—even hitting occasional home runs. For Dee, that's the greatest reward of all, and he sometimes attends Terry's baseball games.

"To run and play ball and feel good, it's just unbelievable," Terry says. "It's just fantastic. Well, it *is* a miracle."

"You had a good game tonight," comments Dee, walking off the baseball field with Terry and Kathy. "To see him enjoy life the way that he was planning on doing before he had gotten sick," says Dee, "puts a real good feeling in your heart."

"Dee is just everything to me," says Terry. "You just can't repay somebody that does something like that. But you can be there if he needs help, and you can just be his friend. And that's what I'm trying to be."

"There's a bond there that can't be broken," confirms Kathy. "Terry is two people. He's Dee and Terry together. And that will be forever."

$\mathcal{D}$IVINE DONATION

Like all young newlyweds, Joe and Nancy Mayor of North Jackson, Ohio, were looking forward to the future—not knowing that their future would involve a serious life-threatening illness.

"Nancy developed a strep throat, and it fell down to her kidneys," explains Joe. "At that time, it was very minute. But over the past fifteen years, I could just see her getting sicker and sicker."

"It was arthritic-like symptoms, and my bones ached. Every step I took was painful," says Nancy.

There were times when Joe had to carry his wife downstairs to the couch, and by 1999, there were days when Nancy couldn't function on her own.

"She just didn't have the stamina to stay up any longer," recalls Joe. "Her health just kept dwindling and she got down to eighty-two pounds, about a thirty percent drop in weight."

"I was devastated. I was in shock. It just couldn't be happening to me," says Nancy.

Nancy's kidneys were failing. With few options left, the Mayors met with St. Elizabeth Hospital's kidney transplant coordinator, Megan Begala.

"Nancy was very motivated; she really wanted to get on our waiting list," says Megan. "We told her at that time that the waiting period was usually close to three years. Nancy replied, 'I don't think I can make it that long.'

"I was feeling so sick at the time," recalls Nancy, "I didn't know if I had that kind of time."

"I told Nancy that if she had a live donor, that would make it quicker," says Megan. "However, she didn't have any live donors at that time, and we ended up listing her on the transplant waiting list, probably in September of 1999."

Nancy's family members were tested as potential donors, but no one was compatible. As the months of waiting dragged on, Nancy's health continued to deteriorate.

"She got to the point where she just physically did nothing. She ended up in a wheelchair," says Joe.

"So then I realized, you know, it's not gonna get better," Nancy admitted. "It's gonna get worse."

All Joe and Nancy could do was hold on and pray for a miracle . . . never suspecting that just across town, at Cindy and Norbert Moran's house, their prayers would be heard.

"Norb happened to be sitting on the couch with the paper, and the TV was on," Cindy remembers. "And the TV show that came on was on the PAX channel—it was *It's a Miracle.*"

The story being profiled on the show that day concerned bone marrow transplants, and Cindy says, "The reason that caught my attention is we had just heard, three or four days before, that Nancy was not doing well, and that she was on a transplant list for a kidney." Though Norbert and Cindy were distantly related to Joe, they never thought that they might be able to help Nancy themselves, until a doctor on the program mentioned that sometimes the best match for potential donors isn't necessarily the patient's relatives.

"That was the first time that I became aware that you could be a nonrelated donor for a kidney," says Cindy. "Both Norb and I were like, maybe *we* can help Nancy out.

"I thought it was pretty strange, though, that this program was on right about the time we heard Nancy wasn't doing well. So, we thought that was kind of a miracle, you know," reveals Cindy, laughing. Following the show, she was motivated to log on to the Internet to find out more about nonrelated donors. "After I saw the program, the first thing I did is, I went up and got on the computer to research the statistics on it, and to see how people did who were not related."

What Cindy found on-line encouraged her to go to the next step. "Every single person on the Internet who had been through this considered it to be a very positive experience," Cindy says, and so she arranged for her and her husband to be tested.

It didn't take long for the news to reach Nancy.

"It was just such a sense of relief," Nancy says. "My husband and I were so thrilled, but we knew that there was a long road ahead with the testing process, and so we were just hopeful, and we prayed."

The day finally arrived when Norb and Cindy received the results of their tests from Megan Begala.

"I have some good news and some bad news," Megan told them.

"Bad news first," Cindy insisted.

"Okay, well, the bad news is that, Norb, we really can't use you as a donor because of your age."

"Well, what about my blood?" inquired Cindy.

"Well, that's the good news. You *are* compatible with Nancy. And in fact, your blood not only likes each other, it loves each other," said Megan.

"I can give her a kidney? I can be a donor?" asked Cindy. "That's wonderful.

"I was never afraid to do it," recalls Cindy. "She needs a kidney. I have a kidney. She can have it."

Cindy was thrilled with the news, but compatibility was only the first step. Was she in good enough health to actually go through with the surgery?

"They proceeded with the testing," says Cindy. "And that's when we started to run into some problems."

Cindy's first battery of tests came back abnormal. Her doctors suggested that she change her diet, and scheduled another test for two weeks later.

"And then I have another test done . . . and it's abnormal again," says Cindy. "I was worried that they'd say,

'Okay, that's it, you have an abnormal test, we're not going to go any further.' "

As the weeks of testing dragged on, Nancy did her best to remain strong. But it wasn't easy. "It was a nightmare," she confesses. "I was just afraid because I didn't know what the next day would bring."

Sadly, the step Nancy had hoped to avoid—kidney dialysis—became her only means of staying alive.

"My husband had to do the exchanges for me at home," says Nancy, "and I was afraid that this was gonna be the way my life was gonna be. And it just horrified me. I hated the thought of it."

"In the middle of all this testing, while all this was going on, is when I ran into Nancy at her nephew's and my grandson's joint birthday party," says Cindy. "And Nancy probably would not normally have come to this particular party because she was not feeling well. But she came because she knew I was gonna be there."

"I just couldn't believe that someone who didn't really know me that well would give of herself so much," recalls Nancy. "I was just overwhelmed."

Joe says, "I told my wife she was so lucky, because there's not many people out there that would even think about giving their kidney to somebody like that."

Finally, after weeks of delays, Cindy was cleared for donation, and surgery was scheduled for October 16, 2000. With her life-saving angel only a few doors away from her at the hospital, Nancy took the opportunity to thank and embrace Cindy again.

"By the time we got in the hospital, we were so relieved; nobody was remotely upset about having the surgery done. We're like, Oh, my God, we made it, we got here, whew. You know, the worst is done," recalls Cindy.

"It was like, you know, reaching the top of the mountain," says Nancy. "You know, we had gotten there." A few last-minute fears remained, however, which she expressed to Cindy before their surgery, saying, "I just think it's impossible. I keep waiting for something else to happen."

"Look, tomorrow you'll have one good kidney. And I'll have one good kidney," Cindy reassured her.

But it wouldn't be that simple.

The transplant required two surgical teams and two operating rooms: Nancy in one and Cindy in the other. Cindy's operation to retrieve the donor kidney would start first.

But as Cindy's doctor, Dr. Charles Modlin, began harvesting her kidney, he discovered a virtual time bomb inside her: a renal artery aneurysm. One of Cindy's veins was so thin that at any moment it could have torn and she would have bled to death.

"I was impressed with the size of the aneurysm, how thin-walled it was, and I said to my assistants, 'I think it's a good thing that this was discovered,'" recalls Dr. Modlin. "Any minor trauma may have caused this aneurysm to perforate. Cynthia might have lost her life from this."

Dr. Modlin and the team of surgeons continued with the procedure to remove Cindy's kidney. "Following the closure of her incision," says Dr. Modlin, "I proceeded to operate on the kidney on the back bench table and dissect out the renal artery aneurysm."

The renal artery now repaired, Dr. Modlin and Dr. Cindy Smetanka, Nancy's doctor, transplanted the donor kidney into Nancy Mayor.

"Overall, both the donor and the recipient did well, without any undue effects from the aneurysm," states Dr. Smetanka.

The surgery was a success, and Nancy was on her way to a full recovery. But Cindy was still in for the shock of her life.

"The next morning, Megan was the first person I saw," says Cindy. "She came in and, you know, I asked her how Nancy's doing, and she said, 'Nancy's doing great, but I just can't believe how this surgery worked out for both of you.' She said, 'I need to tell you that they found an aneurysm on your renal artery.'

"And I'm like, that's nice. They fixed that. But she's going, 'No, you don't understand. This was a life-threatening aneurysm,'" recalls Cindy.

"You could have died, Cindy," her husband, Norbert, told her. "We're lucky you're alive." Looking back on it, Norbert says, "She could've stumbled going up a step, tripped on a stone, fallen down, and the thing would have ruptured and she'd be gone."

"It was so mind-boggling," says Cindy. "It was like, it wasn't scary even. It was just... I should have been gone. Ya know?"

Later, when Nancy and Cindy met face-to-face, the enormity of what had happened finally hit them.

"Thank you for saving my life," said Cindy, as soon as she saw Nancy. Confused, Nancy replied, "Saving *your* life?

"That's when I first realized that this was a double miracle," explains Nancy. "It had saved both of our lives.

It's difficult to say what might have happened if Cindy hadn't chanced on *It's a Miracle*, or if the story of a non-related donor transplant hadn't been featured that day. But it was also her determination to continue in the face of abnormal tests that ultimately kept the miracle alive. It was as if somehow it was meant to be.

And today, months after their surgeries, Cindy and Nancy can honestly say that they owe each other their lives.

"The transplant recipient is in a position where they feel like, 'What am I ever gonna do to pay you back?' Obviously, the person donating never wants them to feel like that," says Cindy. "But in this case, this is the perfect payback. She saved my life too."

"Since the transplant, I think about Cindy all the time," Nancy confesses. "She's always in my prayers. Every time I talk to her it's a new realization of how blessed I am. It's amazing."

She adds, "I believe it's a miracle."

$\mathcal{A}$ SWIMMER'S HEART

In 1988, Gaea Shaw of Denver, Colorado, received a horrifying phone call from her sister Joanne. Joanne had been diagnosed with cardiomyopathy, a deadly and hereditary disease of the heart. Her prognosis was bleak and, eventually, Joanne died.

Gaea says, "My sister's death was totally devastating. I loved her so much. It was such an enormous loss for me... and it was coupled with the awareness that this could be me."

A visit to her doctor confirmed Gaea's fears. Her heart was slowly deteriorating, just as Joanne's had. By 1993, Gaea began exhibiting symptoms of her condition. She describes how her disease became truly life-threatening: "I was reading in bed and suddenly I couldn't breathe. And when I stood up to walk across the room I could barely walk."

Gaea's husband, Barry, rushed her to the doctor. He recalls, "Our life changed in a flash, literally. Gaea was hospitalized. She was told by her medical doctors that she would need a heart transplant within a five-year period. And we absolutely took that very, very hard."

Over the next five years, Gaea carefully guarded her health, even trying experimental medications to improve her heart function. But nothing seemed to help. There was only one option left, and Dr. Eugene Wolfel broke the difficult news. He told Gaea, "I really think it's time to seriously consider going on with the heart transplant evaluation."

Dr. Wolfel explains, "Transplantation is a big step medically and psychologically for patients. When I talked with Gaea in the past about this, she was somewhat reluctant to consider this option. But finally Gaea admitted that she felt so poorly that indeed she had resigned herself that this was the next step in the treatment of her cardiomyopathy."

Gaea was given a pager so that she could always be reached in the event a suitable heart was found. Knowing that she could die at any moment, Gaea waited and prayed... until finally, four months later, the pager went off.

Gaea says, "I looked down and I said, 'This is it. This is the call.'"

"They said, 'Yes, we have a heart for you,'" Barry continues. "'We'd like you to be down here within an hour.'"

"We were told only that it was the heart of a fifteen-year-old boy who lived in the mountains. And that's all we knew," says Gaea.

The boy's name was Christopher Kuhlman, the victim of a tragic car accident. His parents, George and Joni Kuhlman, had agreed to terminate life support and donate their son's organs. It was a difficult decision.

Joni remembers those anxious moments in the hospital. "We kept asking them if there was anything they could do in surgery, if there's a miracle that could happen that could bring him around."

Joni asked the doctors "if we sat there and just talked to him for a really long time, if he would just wake up. We were just really begging them to do anything that would bring Christopher back to normal again. But that didn't happen."

As Gaea was prepped for surgery, her husband and daughter said what could have been their final good-byes. Then Gaea was wheeled into the O.R., leaving her family to wait.

Says Barry, "I have never, ever experienced a good-bye like that in my life. It was an explosion of love, an explosion of total not knowing. I was imagining, Oh, my God, they are going to saw my wife's chest open, take out the only heart she has ever known, put another heart in. Then wait for this moment of truth, whether this heart will start up and beat.

"The nurse came out after surgery and said, 'She got the most beautiful heart I have seen in a transplant surgery.'"

Gaea had been given a second chance at life, thanks to the sacrifice of fifteen-year-old Christopher Kuhlman. And her new heart was filled with emotion.

"You know, to be at death's door and to be told you're going to get your life back," a now-healthy Gaea says. "Those are words that are magical. I knew that for my donor's family, their grief must be enormous. And that it was only because of their generosity that I've been given a second chance at life."

Gaea was determined to make the most of that chance. She began a rigorous rehabilitation program. But there was a problem.

Gaea explains, "Although my heart was fifteen and I had all of that wonderful energy, my body was deconditioned from so many years of not doing anything. So everything I did hurt.

"But somehow I got the idea maybe I could swim. And I said, 'If I can go swimming, will you let me go swimming? And I will do that as an alternative to the rehab care.' And they said, 'Sure, go see if you like it.'"

So Gaea began a regimen of swimming. "The first time I went to the pool," she remembers, "I swam for forty minutes without stopping. I felt like a dolphin. I could have screamed, I was so excited."

Barry tells us what made this experience so unusual. "Before that, Gaea had only recreationally swum. It quickly, mysteriously became a passion."

Gaea agrees. "It was so magical. Once I started swimming it became so clear to me that that is what I was meant to do."

It was at that time that Gaea first learned of the U.S. Transplant Games.

"I found out that there were competitions for people who'd had transplants," she says. "I got pretty excited. I called to find out and I said, 'I'm really pretty much a couch potato level of swimmer; is it okay for me to go?' And they said, 'Absolutely.' "

Gaea began training for the Games with the help of lifeguard Liz Kaplan. Liz noticed while coaching her that "Gaea had a lot of enthusiasm. And she wanted to learn quickly. I was very surprised how quickly Gaea took to the water. There was something within her that made her a very eager, quick-learning student."

After four months of training, Gaea competed in the 1998 U.S. Transplant Games. To everyone's surprise, she took the gold medal in her first event.

Gaea reflects on this accomplishment, saying, "The medal was great. It was fun to take it home and show it off. But the true gold was being alive. And in my way of thinking, everyone at the Games was a gold medal winner. All of us were there only because somebody in the depth of their grief made the decision to donate their loved one's organs so that we could be alive."

Gaea had come back from the brink of death to become a champion. But her miraculous journey was only beginning. When the Shaws returned home, they felt compelled to write the family of her donor and express their eternal gratitude.

Gaea's letter read:

To the family of my heart donor,

You have been in my thoughts and prayers so many times. I cannot imagine anything more painful than losing a child. I feel so profoundly blessed to have received his

heart and there are no words to adequately express my
gratitude to you for your decision.
>*With love and respect and much appreciation,*
>>*Gaea Shaw*

The letter soon made its way to Joni and George Kuhlman, who were still trying to cope with the loss of their son Christopher. As Joni remembers, "There was so much appreciation. So much gratitude. And so heartfelt, it helped with the grieving. But it was very sad just knowing that Christopher was gone."

Joni decided to answer the letter with a package that contained photos and memories of her beloved son. She and her family went through their albums, selecting just the right mementos to send to Gaea. *Now it is time,* Joni wrote in her letter, *with pride and love to introduce you to the wonderful child who helped you.*

Joni describes the rest of the letter: "In the letter, I told them that Christopher was very bright. And that he was in a lot of big accelerated programs. And that he loved to play tricks on his brother. And he loved the beauty of the outdoors and he was always really happy."

And from the letter came a miraculous connection.

Gaea learned that "Christopher loved to go swimming. He was definitely comfortable being in the water. That was such a wonderful connection. That was perfect."

From the exchange of letters, the Shaws and the Kuhlmans began to form a close bond. And in February of 1999, the Kuhlmans finally felt ready to meet the woman who now embodied their son's heart.

When they met, Joni recalls, "I just ran up to her and hugged her and didn't want to let go. It was just wonderful to finally meet this person that had Christopher's heart."

Gaea says, "My heart was pounding so fast from the excitement." And she gave Joni the best gift she could have.

"She let me put my ear right up against her chest," Joni says. "It was a nice strong heartbeat. And it just made things right."

Through Christopher's heart, these two families were now forever intertwined. Together they attended the 2000 Transplant Games, so the Kuhlmans could see first-hand what had been accomplished through their miraculous gift.

For Joni, "It was just incredible to cheer her on and to see her work so hard at competing when she was so sick just such a short time before. I was really very proud of Gaea because she had worked very hard.

"But all I could think about was Christopher swimming and being all silly. And so it was hard to see that. But it was really wonderful to see what can happen when someone gets a second chance. Even though Christopher's not here, he is still carrying on."

The Kuhlmans' presence at the Games was equally important to Gaea. "I know that I swam faster because they were there. They were the inspiration for me."

Gaea knows that she will carry Christopher's gift with her forever.

"This is a miraculous thing," she says. "I don't think it's

any coincidence that I started loving swimming after I got the heart of a person who loved swimming. Sometimes when I'm swimming and I'm pushing hard, I'll say, 'Help me out here, Christopher!'

"He's always with me. I feel that . . . deeply."

DIVINE INTERVENTION

MIRACLE ON THE SKI LIFT

Don and Suzanne Templeton of Albuquerque, New Mexico, have always been avid skiers. It's a love they've passed down to their children.

"Donny started when he was about two," Don remembers. "And then Adrienne started when she was about three years old. She and Donny are different. He's more laid-back. She's more gung ho."

"Adrienne is a very determined girl," adds Suzanne. "She's very competitive. It doesn't bother her a bit that she's the only girl on the all-boys' hockey team. She's pretty wild. She likes to have fun."

In January 2001, the Templetons joined Adrienne's

cousins, Miles and Curtis Maynard, and their parents, Mark and Jane, for a weekend on the slopes.

"Jane doesn't like to ski so I decided not to ski that day," says Suzanne. "So Don and Mark took the kids up skiing."

But before they headed up the mountain, Don and Mark instructed the children in what to do if they got separated.

Don recalls, "We said if we get separated for whatever reason, we'll meet at the bottom of this chairlift at eleven-thirty. I wanted Adrienne to ride up with Mark 'cause she's the littlest, but she wanted to go with Donny and Curtis and Miles, so I said, 'Okay, we'll meet you at the top.' The plan was that we were gonna ski together. What happened was, they were about seven or eight chairs ahead of us. Before we got off the chair we saw them take off. That's where we got separated."

But Don and Mark weren't that concerned. They knew that their children were all good skiers. Even at the ripe old age of seven, little Adrienne had been skiing for years. When they reached the bottom of the run, they decided to get right back on the lift. Adrienne was standing next to her cousin Curtis when things began to go wrong.

Curtis explains, "We got on, and she had gotten on kinda funky, I guess. Her butt wasn't fully on the seat or something. And when I looked over to her, she was sliding off, so I grabbed onto Adrienne. I was holding on to her as hard as I could. I didn't wanna drop her or anything."

Desperate to keep his sister from falling, Donny grabbed for her other hand.

Donny remembers, "And then she's like, 'Don't let go of me. Pull me up!' We're trying to pull her up, but we're sitting down. It's really hard to pull things up. All that equipment's really heavy, and her glove was slipping off. Her glove slipped off and Curtis was just holding on with all his might."

As twelve-year-old Curtis rallied all his strength to hold on, the chairlift continued to climb the mountain.

"I was like, I wish my dad and my uncle were here," says Donny.

The two men were on their way back down the hill when Mark spotted something in the distance.

"As I looked down the slope below me, I noticed a child dangling from a chair. From the height involved, I could tell that death was a real possibility for the child."

Don came down the slope just after Mark, and heard the commotion.

"I could hear somebody yelling that there's a little girl in trouble. And I was hoping, 'God, I just pray that's not Adrienne.' And then I just started noticing it looked like her, and I realized it was her."

Suddenly the chairlift stopped, leaving little Adrienne dangling over forty feet above the ground.

"I just felt so helpless," recalls Don. "I felt like I just possibly cost my little girl's life because I wasn't up there with her."

Curtis remembers, "I was yelling, 'I can't hold her!

Can't hold her any longer.' My fingers were getting numb from holding on to her for so long. I couldn't help it. She was too heavy and fell."

Don saw it all. "I just thought, Oh, my God. She hit like a rag doll. And her helmet popped off her head and was rolling down the hill. We didn't know how much damage was done to her. I was just praying that all she did was break her leg. If all she did was break her leg, I'd be thankful."

As the ski patrol evaluated Adrienne's condition, the boys watched from above.

"We weren't sure if she was alive or not. We just saw her hit the ground. I was trying to tell my cousin that she was okay because he was crying," says Curtis. "And we were all crying. We were very scared."

But no one was more terrified than Don Templeton as he watched the ski patrol prepare to take his daughter back down the mountain.

"To have to be witness to something like that happening to your child, and being totally helpless. I mean, I was worried—my God, she could have had a neck injury. We didn't know yet if her leg was broken or if she had a spinal injury."

Adrienne was rushed to a nearby hospital, where another surprise was waiting. Miraculously, after a fall of forty-three feet, she suffered not one single injury.

Don recalls with wonder, "The X rays and CAT scans hadn't shown any problems and we were able to walk out of there without even a broken leg."

That evening, everyone was safe at home and life was back to normal.

"Normal is everything," says Don. "You don't realize how good it is to be back to normal. We take so much for granted. Somebody's life, especially your own child's. For me, that's everything."

"What happened that day was a miracle," says Suzanne. "We could have lost her in an instant. Adrienne would be no more. And yet, she walked away without a scratch, without a bruise. It's just amazing."

And what is even more amazing are the circumstances that combined to save her life.

Mark explains, "It's truly a miracle that the kids on the chair could have held her like they did. We think that they held on to her for about five minutes. About two minutes' worth of moving lift and another three of stopped lift. And it was particularly fortuitous that they did, because if she had landed fifty yards farther down, she would have been on flat cementlike snow. If she had landed seventy-five yards farther up, it would have been on rocks."

"I think that it's a miracle that falling that far she didn't get hurt," marvels Curtis.

Adrienne put it best, "When I fell off the chairlift, God was watching over me. He just laid me down softly."

SECOND SIGHT

On October 9, 1990, thirty-year-old Renay Poirer was working as a senior maintenance electrician at a computer company near Eau Claire, Wisconsin, when a massive power outage hit the entire complex. It was left to Renay, his supervisor, and a coworker, Steve Eichinger, to repair the problem.

"I had gone to work alone on one electrical box, and Renay and my supervisor decided to start on another one," says Steve. "Everyone believed that the power was off."

But they were wrong.

In an instant, one hundred thousand volts of electricity would change Renay's life forever.

Steve was working three hundred feet away when all of a sudden, he says, "I heard a loud cracking and popping sound." It was the cracking of electricity—which left Renay badly electrocuted.

"Immediately, I knew something horrible had happened. I was very afraid going up there," says Steve, as he ran to help Renay. "I had butterflies in my stomach. I mean, it felt like my stomach had sunk."

When he reached Renay, Steve's immediate concern was whether his coworker was all right. Luckily, Renay was alive. But as Steve recalls, "He indicated then that he could not see."

The world was disappearing for Renay Poirer. He was going blind.

Dr. James Redmann, an ophthalmologist, was brought in to assess the damage. "He did have a few small scratches on the surface of the cornea," says Dr. Redmann. "Small burns, actually. Normally, I would have expected those to clear up within perhaps a week or two, and likewise, I would have expected his vision to clear up also during that period of time."

"I figured that the doctor knew what was going on, and that in a couple of days I'd be back to work. And life would be back on track," says Renay. "But it didn't work out that way."

Renay's vision did not return.

"Renay had us all stumped in terms of an actual reason for the visual loss," recalls Dr. Redmann. "We certainly could not explain it on the basis of a specific eye problem.

So we were left with: Is there some other area of the brain that's affected, that we simply don't know enough about to make a determination?"

With no explanation for his blindness, and little hope that his sight would return, Renay's life was turned upside down.

"In many ways I was like a child. I went through a learning curve with everything I did. It was even hard to walk.... The only way to describe it is like walking in a canoe. I do most of the cooking, and I had to learn to cook again—which turned into a disaster many times," remembers Renay, pausing. "It was very depressing. It was very lonely. It was very scary. It was a horrible, horrible time."

But the cruelest punishment of all was never being able to see his two young daughters. They would grow up without his ever experiencing a father's joy of watching them change.

"It was very difficult for me to accept the fact that I wouldn't be the person taking care of my family. And I wouldn't be the one to see them smile," Renay says, weeping.

"We had no clue as to what the future would bring," affirms Renay's wife, Connie. "We didn't know what he was supposed to do now. Where he was supposed to work. *If* he was supposed to work. And we both knew that at age thirty, he couldn't *not* do anything. He had to find something to do."

But no matter how hard he tried, Renay was unable to hold down a steady job.

And then one day, something unexpected happened.

A man named Mitch flagged down the car that Renay was riding in one day, crying, "Someone call 911! Please! Quickly!"

"What's going on?" Renay asked. Mitch explained that he believed another motorist, a woman, had just suffered a heart attack. "I know CPR," said Renay. "Can you help me get over there? I'm blind." The man assisted Renay over to the woman's car, and Renay immediately went into action. He helped lift the woman out of the car, and began to look for signs of life.

"I couldn't find a pulse. And I couldn't hear her breathe," recalls Renay. "There wasn't anybody else there that said they knew CPR. So I had to do it myself."

Ten minutes later, paramedics arrived and rushed the victim to a hospital. When she was safely out of harm's way, the woman's family invited Renay to visit her so that she could express her gratitude.

"I said, 'I'm the one who should be grateful here, not you. You made me feel like I'm worth something again.' And it was the first time since my accident that I felt good about being me," declares Renay.

Renay's life finally had meaning again, and in the years to follow, he trained to become a physical therapist assistant. He eventually landed a job at Sacred Heart Hospital, where he became friends with the chaplain, Father Klimek.

"My brother was a patient here in the rehab unit, and Renay worked with him very, very closely," says Father Klimek, explaining how he and Renay first got to know one another. Father Klimek was also impressed by Renay's skill with the other rehab patients. "Somehow, through Renay's patience and encouragement, patients were more determined than ever to try to become very independent."

Then, on May 23, 2000, Renay's patience and encouragement was repaid in a way he never expected.

While doing dishes at work, Renay says, "I got a severe headache. It was just a crushing, pounding headache. And it was followed by a brilliant light.

"And then I realized that the trees were moving. I could see the grass. Oh, my God, I can *see!*"

Renay ran straightaway to Father Klimek's church. "I ran down nine flights of steps and down a hall to the chapel, and I dropped to my knees and I started thanking God. Thank you. That was beautiful."

Renay called out to Father Klimek. "I opened the door and there stood Renay, very, very excited," he recalls. "And I said, 'What's the matter?' He said, 'I can see, I can see!' Father Klimek then walked Renay out the front door, and said, 'Renay, go see what you've been missing.'"

"I laid down on my back on the grass and I looked up and I watched the clouds float by," says Renay. "I was very much overwhelmed by everything that had just happened."

Renay rushed home to an empty house, and while he waited for his family to return, he took a moment to look through the family album. It was the first time in ten years that he had seen the faces of the people he loved.

"I was so happy that I could see them. I was studying their faces, and thinking in the back of my mind that if God takes my sight away now, I'd be happy to at least have seen them again."

Today, those who knew him during the years he was blind can offer only one explanation for Renay's sudden return to sight.

"You can call it a miracle. You can call it a special gift of God," says Father Klimek.

"I know in talking with Renay that he views the return of his vision as a gift from God. And I'm inclined to agree with him, because we certainly don't have any other explanation for why it suddenly improved," Dr. Redmann admits.

"I love him more than words can say, and if there was anything I hoped for for him," says Connie, "it was truly for him to get his sight back."

Taking a moment out from playing ball with his family, Renay avows, "I've been given a second chance, and now I'm not going to let a second slip by. I am going to be busy with my family, busy with my friends. I'm going to leave no stone unturned."

BABY HOPE

Raymond and Elizabeth Reyes were married on October 23, 1972. And like other young couples, they dreamed of raising a family. But sadly, as the years passed, they were unable to conceive.

"So the only thing we could do was adopt," remembers Elizabeth. "And that's how we began our process in adoption, adopting our son. It was nice for us to have a boy, but I still wanted a little girl to make our family complete. I started preparing her room by buying a baby crib, and clothes, and stuffed animals."

But the adoption agency was unable to find them a baby girl.

"Days went by. Weeks, months, years went on, but I never gave up hope that someday we would get the baby we always wanted."

And then one day, while working on his garbage collection route, something caught Raymond's eye.

Raymond says, "I was cleaning up alleyways and I saw something that looked like a shrine. I walked up to it, and I saw this folded paper. I grabbed it and opened it up and it was a picture of a saint. I could not believe somebody would throw something like this away. I brought the picture home, and gave it to my wife to give to my mother-in-law, because she collected saints."

When Elizabeth showed the picture to her mother, she learned that the saint might have a very special meaning in her life.

"My mother said that the picture was of Saint Teresa, the saint of babies."

Ray remembers, "I said, 'What do you mean by that?' And she said, 'This picture's gonna bring you the little girl you wanted.'"

"When we first got the picture we framed it and hung it in the baby's room," says Elizabeth. "I would always look at the picture and say, 'How much longer is it going to take?'"

Two weeks later, another man—Roy Grammar—was leaving for work when he noticed a man lurking near some garbage cans.

"He was kind of suspicious-looking. It seemed as if he were looking for something. I stopped to ask him what or who he was looking for. 'What are you doing here?' I asked. And that's when he pointed to the garbage can. I started walking back toward the can. I heard something that sounded like a small kitten or cat. And once I opened the lid, nothing came out."

But Roy could still hear the strange sound and so he dug deeper into the garbage, expecting to find a small animal.

"And then all of a sudden, I saw these little fingers wiggling. And that's when I realized that it was a baby. And you could tell that she was only a few hours old. I asked myself, How could somebody do this? There was a mattress leaning up against the fence, so I flipped it down on the ground, laid her down on the mattress, and rolled her up in a sweatshirt so she'd be warm while I called 911, you know, so that I wouldn't be trying to hold her. The lady asked me, 'What's the emergency?' And I said, 'I just found a baby in a garbage can.' And she said, 'We have the ambulances rolling.'"

Moments later, paramedics arrived to take the newborn to a nearby hospital.

Roy remembers, "I told them, 'I found this baby in this trash dumpster here. I thought she was a cat or something. A guy left her.' They just grabbed her and took her . . . and I just thought to myself that I'd probably never see her again. Even though she wasn't my child, I still wanted to know that she was being taken care of."

By now, the local press had picked up the incredible story and everyone in the small town of Guadalupe, Arizona, had heard of the child they were calling "Baby Hope." Everyone . . . including Elizabeth Reyes.

Elizabeth says, "When I first heard the news, I thought, This is the one we've been praying for."

Ray and Elizabeth felt that hearing about the baby in the garbage so soon after finding Saint Teresa's picture was a miraculous sign. And so they called to inquire about adopting the child. Unfortunately, several other families had also called.

Elizabeth says, "Our chances were slim. My husband and I felt that we would not be able to get her because we were poor. I thought that that was going to keep us from getting Baby Hope."

Ray asked, "Is it the money?" And the authorities told him, "No, it's not the money. We aren't worried about the money. It's the love that you have for an adopted baby." "Oh, there's plenty of that in our house," Ray told them.

And seven days later, they received the call they'd been praying for.

"One of the board members said, 'Let the Reyes family adopt Baby Hope,'" Ray recalled. "And that was our chance. Our prayers were answered."

"I was so excited about the news," says Elizabeth. "I started getting on the phone to tell everybody the good news: We were going to get Baby Hope."

The next day, Elizabeth and Ray arrived at the hospital to meet their new daughter.

Such a special child deserved a special name.

Elizabeth says, "We decided to keep Hope as Esperanza

in Spanish, and to give her the middle name Teresa for Saint Teresa, the saint who helped us."

Ray says, "I believe that Santa Teresa was pretty much involved in us adopting Baby Hope. It's a miracle from Santa Teresa to have done what she did for us."

Elizabeth and Ray did not forget the man who found Baby Hope. And when Esperanza was six months old, they contacted him.

"I got a phone call that they wanted to meet me," Roy remembered. "And they said they had something they wanted to give me for Christmas. When they arrived, that was a pretty exciting moment. I didn't expect to ever see her again. So you know it has to be a miracle."

From that first meeting, Roy became like an uncle to Esperanza. He visits her every year on her birthday.

"They're doing a great job raising her," he says. "And I feel privileged that they've allowed me to even be a part of it."

It's been a long journey for Elizabeth and Ray since they first dreamed of having a daughter. And they have no doubt that she was brought to them by a miracle.

Elizabeth says, "When my husband found the picture of Saint Teresa, that was the answer to our prayers in having Esperanza with us. I feel that this is a miracle. We never would have gotten her if it wasn't for that picture of Saint Teresa."

Ray says, "She had to be meant for us. Somebody answered our prayers."

THANKSGIVING ANGEL

The year was 1969. Ivy Olson, a recently divorced and struggling young mother, was moving into a modest one-bedroom apartment with her two sons. Money was tight, and Ivy had trouble making ends meet...even with her job in a doctor's office. Her situation became particularly troubling during the holidays.

"One of the hardest Thanksgivings I have ever had was the Thanksgiving after I was divorced," recalls Ivy. "Waking up for Thanksgiving realizing that nobody had invited us to their home, the only food we had in the home was three hot dogs, and it was an overwhelming feeling of, What have I gotten into, and how am I going to get out of this? I was down. I really felt despair."

Ivy put on a brave face for her children and took them to a local park, hoping that the boys would have a fun day, even if they couldn't have a real Thanksgiving dinner. She took the hot dogs with her and cooked the only food they had while the boys played at the park.

"Coming back from our little picnic, though," says Ivy, "I can remember the boys saying, 'Mom, we're so hungry.' And I knew there was absolutely no money, no food, nothing. I don't think I've ever felt so all alone as I did coming back, wondering, How are we going to do this? How am I going to do this?"

But as she started up the stairs to her apartment, something incredible occurred.

"This little old lady came out of the bottom apartment," recounts Ivy, "and she says, 'Oh, honey, I cooked Thanksgiving dinner for you and the boys.' And I looked at her. . . . I'd never seen her before. . . . It was just a complete stranger."

"Oh, no, we couldn't impose," Ivy protested when the woman insisted that they come eat. But the woman was so insistent that they join her for dinner that Ivy couldn't refuse.

The woman's invitation was a prayer answered. Entering the apartment, Ivy felt immediately at home. Thanksgiving dinner was laid out on the table waiting for them.

"Wow, this is great," the kids exclaimed.

"It was all dimly lit," describes Ivy, "and the kitchen table was just loaded with food, and she was just so incredibly sweet."

The woman carved the turkey, and they all began to eat and enjoy each other's company.

"Her presence was like electricity," says Ivy. "She had a sparkle in her eyes. There was life in her. You know how in the presence of some people you feel absolutely comfortable? That was what she created that evening for us. Food, yes, lots of it, but for me and the loneliness that I felt, what she gave me was unconditional love . . . and it was just one of the most special evenings that I have ever spent in my whole life."

As Ivy and her sons were leaving, the neighbor presented them each with a gift. But they also left with something they desperately needed.

"Food!" exclaims Ivy. "Loads of leftovers. I mean, we had food for a week. If you can compare how I started that morning with that total feeling of despair and loneliness, and not being good enough, to ending up feeling, I'm okay. I'm worthwhile. I'm a good mom. It was a miracle."

The unexpected act of kindness had given her a new lease on life. But the next day, Ivy was in for an even bigger surprise. This Thanksgiving was not just a random act of kindness by a thoughtful neighbor.

"I got all my empty containers," explains Ivy, "to take them downstairs to my new friend. And I went down there and knocked on the door, and there was no answer. And I looked through the windows, and the place was absolutely dark, and not one piece of furniture was in there. I mean, even today I get goose bumps when I think back on just seeing that empty, empty apartment. And it was like, Uh-oh, something's going on here."

Shocked and confused, Ivy immediately contacted the apartment manager.

"Where's the little old lady that was in that apartment?" Ivy asked.

"Number fifteen's been vacant for ten or twelve weeks now," the manager replied.

"And," adds Ivy, "I said to him, 'No, you don't understand, I had dinner there last night.... Thanksgiving dinner.' And he gave me this weird look, like maybe I should be in an institution or a hospital."

Ivy stared in shock at the manager, remembering the events from the night before.

"I can remember just looking at him," Ivy says, "absolutely knowing that a miracle had happened in my life. And I just thanked him, turned around, and walked up those steps to my apartment."

As she returned home, Ivy began going over the events of the previous evening in her mind, and suddenly she realized that the woman had known personal things about her that she couldn't possibly have known. Like her favorite food—potato salad—and the fact that she worked in a doctor's office.

"I often wonder," admits Ivy, "why I didn't pick up at the actual dinner that this was an angel. I think one of the most important things about my dinner with an angel is that out of my fifty-seven years of living on this earth, that one hour of being loved unconditionally has changed my life so drastically. Can you imagine what it would be like if us earth angels gave some of that unconditional love away? It can make a total difference in people's lives."

911 ANGEL

It was December 5, 1996, Fire Safety Week in Grand Junction, Colorado, and the Genesis Preschool had organized a field trip for their class of three-year-olds to tour the local firehouse.

Firefighter David Austin was in charge that day.

"I just like to walk through between the trucks, show them what the different parts are, the fire hoses, and whatnot. I try and tell the kids not to be afraid of the firemen," he says.

When it came time to teach the children about the importance of dialing 911, three-year-old Britny McElfresh showed a special interest.

"It's never too early for them to learn 911, and how to contact emergency services," declares David. "I explain to them that 911 is not a toy. It's only for emergencies. I'll use a scenario like, What if you find Mom and you can't wake her up? What number are you going to dial? 9–1–1."

For young Britny, the lesson learned that day would soon become the difference between life and death.

A few days later, 911 dispatcher Kendra Andrews answered a call. "When the call first came in I heard some silence. And then I heard a little girl or a small child talking, repeating what I was saying to her," recalls Kendra. The caller was Britny. Her mother was lying on the floor, unconscious and bleeding from the head.

"9–1–1?" asked Britny.

"9–1–1. Can I talk to your mom?" asked Kendra.

"She's got a little sick on her head," said Britny. "She hurt her head."

"She sounded very concerned and anxious," Kendra remembers. "A lot of calls with little kids, you can tell when they're playing on the phone. And she was not, she was very calm and very sincere about what she was telling me."

Britny told Kendra her name, and Kendra inquired, "Brit, where's your mom at?"

"She's right here," Britny said. Kendra then heard her ask, "Mommy...are you okay?"

"At that point I really realized that Mom was not going to come to the phone," says Kendra.

"Does she need an ambulance?" Kendra asked. Britny

replied that she did, and Kendra immediately dispatched an emergency unit to the scene.

"You have to come over and get her and you then have to fix her head," insisted Britny.

"Is she bleeding?" Kendra inquired.

"Yeah, she bleed on her head," replied Britny.

"How much is she bleeding?" Kendra asked. "I was getting very nervous," she recalls, "because I didn't know what had happened." She continued with her line of questioning, and tried to piece together what had occurred. "Is your mom breathing, do you know?"

"No, she died a while back," said Britny.

"She died?" repeated Kendra, surprised. "That really concerned me, when she kept insisting that her mom had died. At one point, I really got very nervous that maybe that might have happened," says Kendra. "I cannot imagine a three-year-old looking at their mom, and wondering, and really saying that she was dead. It must have been very scary for her."

It was at that point that Kendra learned that there was someone else in the house.

"It looks like a silly man," said Britny.

"She talked about a silly little man that was in the room with her," Kendra says, "and I wasn't sure what she was talking about, if there was another person in the house who may have done this to her mom, who had come back to do some more to her mom." Kendra then asked Britny where her father was. "Part of the reason I asked if Dad was around was to see if *he* was the silly-looking man she was talking about, or if Dad could help. And she told me, no, that he was at work." Assessing the situation, Kendra states, "There very well could have been a perpetrator in the house."

Soon after, volunteer paramedic Lee Hyde rode up on his motorcycle. He was the first to arrive on the scene. He tried the front door of the house but found it locked, and Britny refused to answer his knocking.

"I could just kind of barely see the mom through the window. It was kind of a difficult angle to see," recalls Lee. "The little girl would not let me in the house. I was a stranger to her, and she was not gonna let me in. But she was on the phone with 911 dispatch."

Moments later, the rest of the paramedic team arrived. Luckily, David Austin was among them. Britny recognized the man who'd taught her to dial 911, and finally opened the door.

"I was very relieved once the rescue squad got there, because I knew my job was over, and the people that needed to be on the scene were there," says Kendra.

From evidence at the scene, the rescue squad was able to piece together what had happened: While feeding her children breakfast, some baby food had spilled on the floor, causing the young mother to slip. She'd hit her head during the fall. Her condition was serious; she had already lost a great deal of blood, and her brain had begun to swell.

"It was a very good thing that the little girl called 911 when she did, because the longer a head injury goes without being treated, the worse it can be," explains Lee Hyde.

"She could have possibly had a stroke, or been brain-dead in a matter of hours."

Robin McElfresh, Britny's mother, was rushed to the hospital, where she was diagnosed with a severe concussion and treated for her injuries. When her husband, Lee McElfresh, arrived, they both learned what a brave and miraculous thing Britny had done.

"When they told us our daughter, three and a half years old, had dialed 911, my wife and I were both in disbelief," says Lee.

"When I woke up in the hospital, a nurse came to me and said, 'Wow, your daughter saved your life,' and I said, 'No, I'm sorry, you're wrong,'" recalls Robin. "And they said, 'No, we've got her on tape, it's her.' And I just thought they were wrong. She's only three. She's very little. I just thought it was impossible, but it wasn't."

But just how truly miraculous that day was only became clear when Britny told her parents that "the silly little man" she'd mentioned to the dispatch operator was actually an angel.

"And we said, 'What silly man angel?'" says Robin, "because we hadn't heard anything about this. We said, 'Oh, really? And what did he do?' She said, 'He just kept saying, "Keep telling them, Britny. They'll know, they'll come and they'll help you."' And we said, 'Did he dial 911?' and she said, 'No, I did that myself, and he just helped me not be scared.'"

Robin adds, "I think two or three nights later, the firemen came to our house and gave us a copy of the 911 tape."

The tape only confirmed what Britny knew all along—and even five years later, she remains absolutely convinced of what she saw that day.

"When I told my mom, she did not believe me. And I just said, This really happened, Mom. You have to believe me. I knew what I saw, because I saw it for real," declares Britny.

"There absolutely was an angel watching over Britny. . . . I think there was an angel watching over all of us that day," says Kendra.

"Every day I wake up and thank God that my daughter's here, and that she helped me, and that I'm here. I'm still blown away by it every day. I look at her and I can't believe that, you know, she loved me that much, to really know, to sense that there was something wrong and to take care of it.

"I couldn't be more proud or more in love with that little girl," proclaims Robin.

FATE FIGHTS FIRE

On January 5, 1995, the Windsor Fire Department in Ontario, Canada, received an emergency distress call. Fire-fighters Evan Fournier and Doug Emery were part of the team that responded to the report of a child in jeopardy.

Doug says, "We got a call for a rescue of a baby who was trapped, so we proceeded to the address."

Upon arriving at the scene, sirens blaring, they checked their tools and prepared themselves for the worst. As Evan explains, "On that type of call, you just think of all the possibilities that could happen for a case like that, and work backward when you get there and see what you've got."

But this time, what the firemen saw upon arriving at the apartment was nothing like what they'd expected.

"We found a child with his head stuck in a rocker," Doug says. "The baby didn't seem to be panicking too much. He was just sitting there looking kind of funny with this rocker stuck around his head." Beth Sutton consoled little Nathaniel while the firemen helped to extract him from the rocking chair.

Evan admits, "It was a bit comical, just to see this picture. Boys will be boys, I suppose, and they'll get into all kinds of trouble. I was more than curious as to how this all happened."

Beth recalls, "We were just at home having sort of a regular day. Nathaniel was playing while I was on the phone with my girlfriend, and I just turned around and Nathaniel had his head stuck in the chair!" Although she tried everything she could think of to get her son unstuck from the rocker, she couldn't do it, and eventually called the fire department. However, the successful rescue of Nathaniel was only the beginning.

"While we were there," says Doug, "I noticed that the apartment had no smoke detectors. I asked the mother if she had any, but she didn't because she was only renting the apartment. I told her she really should get some, even if she's renting."

A few months earlier, the Windsor Fire Department had initiated a citywide program to provide residents with free smoke detectors. "The fire department hands them out. We've had so many fires with children that died. It only takes one thing to go wrong, and the mother and child could wind up in trouble in a big hurry."

But Beth didn't take Doug's advice that seriously. "I just thought, Next time I'm at the store I'll pick one up. I didn't feel the need to go out and get one right away."

But the fact that Beth Sutton didn't have an alarm in her apartment continued to bother Doug Emery, Evan remembers. "He mentioned to me that it would be a good idea to get one out there as soon as possible. That caused me to show my boss the report of the call instead of just filing it."

Evan and Doug's boss was District Fire Chief Paul Holmes. When Evan told him about the call to the Suttons' home at 995 Bruce Avenue, Paul checked to be sure Beth knew about the free detector program. "I made a mental note to make sure that if she did not come in the next day and pick up a smoke detector, that the chief or someone from the station would go over and install one."

But something about the situation kept bothering him. "It was almost like there was a hand guiding me, or pushing me—something like that. Firemen don't like to lose people. Two days before, another child had been lost on the east side of the city. I believe that had a lot to do with this sense of urgency." So he made an unusual decision to personally install the detectors right away.

Firefighter Dennis Leslie, who accompanied Paul Holmes, realized immediately that the chief's request was anything but ordinary. "It was very unusual. We usually let fire prevention officers do it, but it was strange—Paul was driven. He just wanted to put it in right there and then."

For the second time that day, the Windsor Fire Department was paying a visit to Beth Sutton's home. Paul and Dennis introduced themselves and explained that they were there to install the smoke detectors. "She said, 'I'm supposed to get one tomorrow,'" Paul recalls. "I don't know if *force* is the right word, but something that was there was telling me to do it, and there was no getting around it, it was going to be done."

The firefighters installed the detectors, explaining them to Beth and Nathaniel. Beth says, "I was actually quite surprised that they came to do that, because I didn't think they did that sort of thing. They left and I hadn't really thought a whole lot about this. I'm like, Okay, whatever."

Later that night at the station, the quiet was pierced by another emergency alarm. Paul noticed the address: "The number registered first, 995, and then Bruce Avenue, and I said to myself, We were just there."

Evan Fournier continues, "I was feeling at that moment that there could be no better crew to investigate this fire than the same people who had been there hours earlier. And I was hoping for the best—that when we arrived there would be a false alarm or it would be something very minor." But Evan's worst fears were realized when the fire trucks raced up to the building. "As it turned out, it wasn't minor at all. There was smoke coming from the apartment and we knew who was in there. We knew the layout of the building."

As they entered the building, the smoke was so thick it was nearly impossible to see. Anyone inside would be asphyxiated within minutes. And every second they spent not locating Beth and her son could mean their certain death.

"After the primary search, I felt that there probably wasn't anybody home," says Evan. "There's still a space or a small room or a closet we could have missed. The mother and the young boy weren't there. They had gone across the street, where she had called 911." Evan rushed to the neighbor's house where mother and child were anxiously waiting, and discovered that they were unharmed. "As soon as I saw Beth and Nathaniel, I was relieved. It was something that thrilled all of us to know that they were both safe. We couldn't have asked for anything better."

The smoke detector had definitely served its purpose earlier that evening.

As to how the fire began, Beth says, "I had put Nathaniel to bed and I went into the kitchen and I was just making myself a little bite to eat. And I thought I had turned the stove off. I was asleep on the couch and I didn't know how long the fire would have been burning, but the smoke detector went off and it woke me up.

"I went into Nathaniel's room, and the first thing I thought about was just grabbing him and getting out of the apartment."

Even though years have passed, Beth and Nathaniel continue to visit the firefighters who, in a strange twist of fate, saved their lives. "Every time I see them I just want to give them each a big hug. I'm so grateful," the lucky mother says with a smile.

And everyone is thankful for the incredible series of events that saved two lives that day. First the freak accident that brought the fire department to 995 Bruce Avenue and alerted them to the fact that no fire alarms were in the apartment. And then, the strange feeling that Chief Paul Holmes couldn't seem to shake, and that brought him back to Beth Sutton's home hours later. It's frightening to imagine what might have happened if all these events had not taken place.

Paul Holmes reflects on the events of that day. "I really feel that something intervened here. It could have been a guardian angel for all I know."

And Beth Sutton agrees. "I am just very thankful that the firemen went with their gut feeling to come back and take the extra time to put the smoke detector in. And definitely, you know, I thank God. I definitely believe that He had a hand in all of it."

Dennis Leslie thinks "it had to be a miracle. There's no doubt in my mind."

GRAND CANYON FALL

Every year the Grand Canyon attracts millions of tourists to experience its awesome beauty. But in 1977, one of those tourists experienced a moment of terror so intense that it still haunts her even today.

Twenty-one years ago, Al Halliday of Hartland, Michigan, took his family on a vacation to Grand Canyon National Park. He brought along his fourteen-year-old sister, Janie.

Janie says, "We stopped off at a lookout point and we were all sort of roaming around on our own."

In spite of warnings posted along the rim, Janie was determined to get a good photograph of the canyon floor, a dangerous shot that could only be taken from beyond the guardrail.

As soon as she stepped past the barrier, her nightmare began.

"I had taken a few photographs just looking out," Janie says, "but I wanted to take one looking down, to show the depth of the canyon. All of a sudden my feet just came out from under me."

Janie hurtled down the steep cliff toward certain death, when suddenly her body came to a mysterious, abrupt stop.

"I just thought, This is strange. What stopped me? There wasn't anything that I did to stop myself. I started shouting for help."

Above her, on the overlook, Janie's family was in a state of shock. They couldn't hear her cries for help and could only imagine that she had fallen thousands of feet.

Al remembers, "My wife was screaming, my sister-in-law was screaming. And I was leaning out, looking over—I couldn't see her, I couldn't even see the bottom. You know, it's one of those moments of sheer panic. What do you do? Where did she go? I yelled her name, but I couldn't hear her answer."

Janie tried to work her way up the steep embankment, but with each movement she risked losing her footing and plunging down the side of the cliff.

"I can remember looking up at the top, but it was so steep!" Janie says. "You couldn't see the top. And I just sat there for a few minutes and thought, How am I supposed to get back up?"

Desperate and frightened, Janie continued to push herself up the steep cliff. But she was in an impossible situation. There was no way that she could save herself on her own.

Janie has no idea how it happened, but one moment she was hopelessly trapped on the side of the canyon, and the next she found herself back at the top.

"I don't remember actually moving up, but I knew something strange had happened. As soon as they saw me, my family just came running, and they were crying, and I was crying... we all just hugged."

When Janie returned home, she shared her terrifying experience with her mother, Shirley. And that's when she discovered a possible explanation for what had happened.

At the exact same moment she was hanging on for her life from the side of the cliff, her mother—over fifteen hundred miles away—experienced a powerful premonition.

"I knew that Janie was going to die," remembers Shirley. "I couldn't stop sobbing."

As quickly as her feeling of panic had arrived, it suddenly left.

"I stopped crying and a peace came over me. And I couldn't imagine why I had this premonition. I didn't even know where Janie and the rest of my family were."

Years later, Shirley traveled to the exact spot where her daughter had nearly died.

"And I walked the trails and went out to the lookout points. Anyone that ever goes over that edge, there is no way they can ever get back to the top without some miracle."

"From that time on," says Janie, "I felt safe, always. I knew that I had a guardian angel that was watching over me."

Today, as Janie prepares to be a mother for the first time, she has no doubt that surviving a fall into the Grand Canyon was nothing short of a miracle.

"My guardian angel is the person that stopped me on that cliff and brought me back up to the top safely. Faith just gets you through every day and every trial and tribulation."

FAMILY RESTAURANT

Lorelei Manning never knew her family. Her father died shortly after she was born, and her mother was too ill to take care of her. Eventually, Lorelei was placed in an orphanage in Manchester, New Hampshire.

"I was about five years old when I went into St. Peter's Orphanage," Lorelei recalls. "I was very much afraid because it was so much space. It was like you were lost in this big, huge building that could have probably swallowed you up. It was very cold. No warmth at all to it. We never got any love from the nuns who ran the orphanage. There was no way of them ever putting their arms around you and saying you're a good girl. There was no love, no love in that place."

It was a lonely place for a young girl who dreamed only of having a family.

"We had what we called visitors that would come in, and it was almost like we were put on display," says Lorelei. "I was hoping someone would take me. And if you weren't picked, you thought, What's wrong with me? Why? You know, why didn't someone pick me?"

Lorelei was never chosen. But it didn't stop her from dreaming.

"I would sit on the swings and look at the clouds and kind of make pictures out of them. And I'd sit there and say, 'Our family is up in heaven. I wonder if my father is in that cloud.' And I truly always wanted his arms around me, just to say things would be okay. Just to have somebody say they love you, you know, and really mean it."

And then, one day, a new girl arrived at the orphanage—Patricia Arnold.

Lorelei was playing alone with a doll. "From the moment I saw Pat when she walked into that playroom, it was like I had to go get her by the hand," Lorelei remembers fondly. "We weren't supposed to get up off our chairs, but I did. And the nun kind of looked at me, and I said, 'Can she come sit with us?' "

Lorelei led Pat to the back of the playroom. "Pat asked if it was my first year there, and I said it was my second. She was afraid," Lorelei says. "I remember her crying, the same as we all did, not knowing where we were or what was going to happen." So Lorelei comforted Pat and told her, "Don't cry, everything is going to be okay. I'll be your friend. Do you want to be my friend?"

From that day on, Pat and Lorelei were inseparable.

"We pretty much talked the same language," admits Lorelei, "and felt emotionally the same. There was food that Pat didn't like that I would eat so she wouldn't get in trouble. For instance, Pat didn't like oatmeal. I'd finish mine and say, 'Okay, when the nun's not looking, pass me your plate!'"

Suddenly, life at the orphanage was no longer lonely or sad.

"We had our fun with waxing the floors and buffing them," Lorelei confesses. "So we'd pretend we were skating or skateboarding or anything, you know, just having our fun. And I remember making beds with her and throwing pillows. Patricia and I became very much like sisters to each other."

Lorelei's dream had finally come true. But sadly, she would wake one day and find Patricia gone. She had been adopted. Once again, Lorelei was on her own.

"I'd get up in the morning and she wasn't there. There were certain things I would still do," Lorelei explains, "but Patricia wasn't there anymore."

When Lorelei turned eighteen, she left the only home she had ever known. By now, the two girls had completely lost track of each other. But Lorelei was determined to find her "sister."

"I went to the library, and they gave me phone books to look at," remembers Lorelei. "I went through phone book after phone book. But the hardest part was that I only had her maiden name—Arnold. She could have married by then, for all I knew."

Lorelei called every number she could, asking for Patricia Arnold, but she had no luck. "I did go back to the orphanage one time," Lorelei says, "and they wouldn't even really let me past the doorway. I asked the woman, 'Don't they have any records left of us? I mean, somebody has to have something.' She said, 'Even if we did, we can't give you that.'

"I went to the church, to St. Joseph's Cathedral, figuring that maybe they could tell me something because we were with the Catholic order. But I found nothing. They couldn't tell me anything. I even looked through obituaries in the newspaper, not hoping to find Patricia's name, but feeling that, maybe if I did, then my search could stop, then the yearning just wouldn't be there...."

But Lorelei never found a clue to Patricia's whereabouts.

"I came up with absolutely nothing. And I just finally said, Let it go," Lorelei says.

After years of desperately searching for her "sister" Patricia and finding no answers, Lorelei Manning went on with her life. She married, raised a family, and eventually settled down in Holiday, Florida. And then on December 7, 1999, while driving with a friend, something truly amazing happened.

"I had a bunch of errands to do," Lorelei recalls, "and I had asked my neighbor, Ruthie, to go with me, figuring, you know, we'd stop and maybe have lunch on the way back."

But none of the restaurants they passed seemed to appeal to Lorelei. And there was also a question of finances.

"I said, 'First, we've got to see what we have in our wallets for money,' because I'm saying lunch and I don't even know what I have. Ruthie had three dollars and I had a five."

They were passing a Bob Evans restaurant, but, with only eight dollars between them, the two women decided to forget about lunch and just head home.

"So we came to this light, and the light changed. I took off, and all of a sudden, right in the front of the parking lot driveway, my steering wheel just jerked right out of my hand." Lorelei thought her steering belt had broken. "I said, 'Ruthie, I've got to get off the road or I'm going to get hit.' I said, 'Here goes nothing,' so I just slowly steered the car into the Bob Evans parking lot and into a spot. I sat there for a minute, and I said, 'Oh, boy. I guess we're here, Ruth. Let's go to lunch.'"

They decided to each order a bowl of soup and split a sandwich.

"The gentleman sitting on the other side of me said, 'Mmm, boy, does that soup smell good!'" Lorelei chatted with the man as she tasted her soup. "So we continued eating and all of a sudden he says, 'Excuse me a second, where are you from?' And I said, 'Holiday, Florida.' And he says, 'No, no, no, no, where are you originally from?'"

When Lorelei told the man that she was from New England, he asked, "Where in New England?"

"Manchester, New Hampshire," Lorelei responded. When the man asked Lorelei what part of Manchester she was from, she told him, "The west side, on Kelly Street.

And then I heard him say to this lady sitting next to him, 'She's from New Hampshire too.'"

The woman leaned over toward Lorelei and repeated, "Manchester?"

"She started to stand up," recalls Lorelei. "I looked over at her, and I said 'Do you know where Kelly Street is?' And she says, 'St. Peter's Orphanage? I grew up at St. Peter's Orphanage.'"

"I grew up at St. Peter's Orphanage too," Lorelei exclaimed. "And I said, 'What's your name?' She says, 'Patricia.' I said, 'Patricia Arnold?' She goes, 'Yeah.' And she looked at me, and I said, 'I'm Lorelei. I'm Lorelei Manning. Oh, my gosh, Patricia, hi!'"

Patricia and Lorelei immediately hugged each other. "And by this time, we're in there hugging each other, crying, and then when we looked around, everyone else was crying on our side," Lorelei recalls her surprise. "I mean, everybody in there was ecstatic. The people that were sitting behind us were clapping. People were going, 'Oh, my God, what a miracle!'"

Pat agrees, laughing, "We had stopped the whole restaurant. They didn't know what was happening. The waitress was ready to call 911!"

After forty-two years, Patricia and Lorelei had found each other again.

Lorelei smiles, "There was such warmth that just came through the both of us, it was like we went back in time to when we were little kids. Time stopped around us for those few minutes. It was, like, this can't be real."

"That was the happiest day of my life," Pat adds without hesitation. "I was so happy. I mean, I had goose bumps. I just...my whole insides were shaking. And then the memories came back from many, many years ago, when we were little girls."

Patricia's memories were bittersweet. She, too, had suffered after being separated from her best friend.

"I missed Lorelei terribly," remembers Pat. "I had nobody to talk to. I sat in my room many nights and cried."

She particularly remembered the last time she had seen Lorelei, on a return visit to the orphanage.

Lorelei ran up to the fence, crying, "Pat's here! Pat's here!" And Pat told Lorelei how much she'd missed her. "I'd grab her hands through the fence," Pat recalls. "We cried. We were lonely, and she asked me 'How you doing, Pat?' 'Not too good.' And I wasn't," Pat admits, crying.

But the bond of love that Pat and Lorelei shared as girls had never weakened. "I never forgot Lorelei," Pat declares. "Never."

"I did wonder if Pat was searching for me, because I had such a strong conviction of it," says Lorelei. "I really thought my feelings were actually going through to her, and I guess I kind of hoped she was saying that maybe I could send her a message if I thought strong enough of her. Maybe she'd think of me...I mean, miracles *do* happen."

"Now I feel I've gotten my sister back," confirms Pat. "And I won't lose her, either."

Since their miraculous reunion in 1999, Patricia has moved to Florida to be near Lorelei. And, like true sisters, they spend their days remembering the past and planning the future.

As they often laugh over old photo albums, Pat might point to a picture and reminisce, "There's Lorelei right there. That's the little girl that said, 'Hi Pat.' That was a long time ago." And Lorelei will join in, "There's Pat right there. Do you remember that?!"

But most of all, they give thanks to the incredible good fortune that brought them back together again.

"The odds of Lorelei and I finding each other were one in a million," Pat emphasizes. "It just doesn't happen every day."

About the Author

RICHARD THOMAS is a highly respected actor who reliably inspires audiences with his versatility. He went professional at age seven, stepping onto the Broadway stage as a young John Roosevelt in *Sunrise at Campobello*. His feature film debut came at sixteen in Universal Studios's *Winning,* starring Paul Newman and Joanne Woodward.

But Thomas stole America's heart with his sensitive portrayal of John-Boy on *The Waltons,* a role that won him a Best Actor Emmy and catapulted him into the spotlight at twenty-one. Since then, he has consistently aligned himself with quality projects, starring in over thirty-eight movies for television, including such classics as *Roots, All Quiet on the Western Front, The Red Badge of Courage, The Homecoming, The Christmas Box,* and many others. His most recent appearance on the big screen was in Paramount Pictures's *Wonder Boys.*

Along with his television work, Thomas is a critically acclaimed star of the theater, having revealed himself over the years to be equally at home in the classics and modern masterpieces. He most recently completed a run on the London stage in the West End production of *Art.*

The actor has taught at universities on behalf of the Kennedy Center's educational programs, served as the National Chairman of The Better Hearing Institute and on the board of The Morris Animal Foundation, and has been honored with a doctor of fine arts degree from the University of South Carolina. He also serves on the board of the Center Theater Group, his theatrical home in Los Angeles.

For his passionate performances, charged with emotional authenticity, Richard Thomas undeniably has become one of America's most revered and beloved talents. As host of *It's a Miracle,* he brings tremendous compassion and joy to chronicling true-life accounts of miraculous events and interventions.

He lives in Los Angeles with his wife, Georgiana, and their children.

Submit your own

to the producers of
PAX TV's *It's a Miracle* at:

Submit Your Miracle
c/o Executive Producer
It's a Miracle
10880 Wilshire Boulevard
Suite 1200
Los Angeles, CA 90024

Or please visit the *It's a Miracle*
website at *www.itsamiracle.tv*